ARIZONA WILDLIFE VIEWING GUIDE

John N. Carr

FALCON PRESS®

ACKNOWLEDGMENTS

As a lifelong resident of Arizona with thirty years' experience as a wildlife biologist for the Arizona Game and Fish Department, I am grateful for this opportunity to share with others the many interesting and scenic areas of my state and the wildlife found here.

Many people contributed to the successful completion of this project and I want to express my thanks and appreciation to all, especially those who nominated viewing sites and reviewed the manuscript. I would like to thank Govenor Fife Symington for his support, and the directors of the Arizona Game and Fish Department, the Bureau of Land Management, the U.S. Fish and Wildlife Service, and the Arizona Department Of Transportation, whose initial efforts got the viewing guide project started.

Special thanks go to Bruce Taubert, Pat O'Brien, and Carolyn Engle-Wilson, Arizona Game and Fish Department; Randall Smith, Coronado National Forest; Ted Cordery, Bureau of Land Management; Frank Baucom and Jim Clark, U.S. Fish and Wildlife Service; Ruth Valencia and Tanna Thornburg, Arizona State Parks; and Dave Schmitt, Arizona Department Of Transportation. Also thanks to Kate Davies of Defenders of Wildlife, who kept me on track; and to John Grassy of Falcon Press, who guided me through the process of writing the manuscript. Thanks to Jim Cole of Wasatch-Cache National Forest in Utah, whose experience and advice got me started in the right direction.

And finally, very special thanks to my wife, Sally: with her help this project was completed on schedule. She went with me to visit every site in this guide, and to many others not selected. In expressing my gratitude, I dedicate this book to her.

Steering Committee:
David L. Schmitt, Arizona Department of Transportation
Ruth Valencia, Arizona State Parks
Frank M. Baucom, U.S. Fish and Wildlife Service
Ted Cordery, Bureau of Land Management
Randall A. Smith, U.S.D.A. Forest Service
Amy L. Heuslein, Bureau of Indian Affairs
Bruce D. Taubert, Arizona Game and Fish Department

Author and State Project Manager:
John N. Carr

National Watchable Wildlife Program Coordinator:
Kate Davies, Defenders of Wildlife

Front Cover Photo:
Antelope ground squirrel, STEPHEN J. KRASEMANN/DRK PHOTO

Back Cover Photos:
Sonoran Desert, Tucson, BRYAN MUNN
Thick-billed Parrot, BOB MILES

CONTENTS

REGION 3 - CENTRAL MOUNTAINS

REGION 4 - WHITE MOUNTAINS

REGION 5 - SKY ISLAND MOUNTAINS

Birdwatching is a very popular family activity at Sabino Canyon Recreation Area near Tucson. DAVED W. LAZAROFF

PROJECT SPONSORS

 DEFENDERS OF WILDLIFE is a national, nonprofit organization of more than 80,000 members and supporters dedicated to preserving the natural abundance and diversity of wildlife and its habitat. A one-year membership is $20 and includes six issues of the bi-monthly magazine, *Defenders*. To join or for further information, write or call Defenders of Wildlife, 1244 Nineteenth St., NW, Washington, DC 20036. (202) 659-9510.

 The ARIZONA GAME AND FISH DEPARTMENT is legally mandated to conserve, enhance, and restore Arizona's diverse wildlife resources and habitats through aggresive protection and management programs, and to provide wildlife resources and watercraft recreation for the enjoyment, appreciation, and use of present and future generations. The Department has management responsibility for all wildlife in the state, including more than 800 native and resident species of mammals, birds, reptiles, amphibians and fish. Arizona Game and Fish Department, 2222 West Greenway Rd., Phoenix, AZ 85023. (602) 942-3000.

 The ARIZONA STATE PARKS BOARD has a mandate to select, acquire, preserve, establish, and maintain areas of natural features, scenic beauty, historical and scientific interest, and zoos and botanical gardens, for the education, pleasure, recreation, and health of the people of the state. Natural, cultural, and recreational state parks can be found at twenty-five locations around the state. The agency is comprised of several other programs including the Statewide Comprehensive Outdoor Recreation Plan, State Historic Preservation Office, State Natural Areas Program, State Trails Program and Heritage Grants Program. Arizona State Parks, 800 West Washington, Suite 415, Phoenix, AZ 85007. (602) 542-4174.

 The BUREAU OF LAND MANAGEMENT is responsible for balanced management of 14.2 million acres of public lands and their various resource values in Arizona, in a combination that will best serve the needs of the American people. Management is based upon the principles of multiple use and sustained yield of resources, taking into account the long-term needs of future generations. The BLM strategic plans *Arizona Wildlife 2000* and *Recreation 2000* help guide the wildlife habitat and recreation initiatives on BLM public lands in the State. Bureau of Land Management, Arizona State Office, 3707 North Seventh Street, Phoenix, AZ 85014. (602) 640-5547.

The FOREST SERVICE, U.S. DEPARTMENT OF AGRICULTURE, has a mandate to protect, improve, and wisely use the nation's forest and range resources for multiple purposes to benefit all Americans. The six national forests of Arizona are sponsors of this program to promote awareness and enjoyment of fish and wildlife on our national forest system lands. USDA Forest Service, 517 Gold Avenue, S.W., Albuquerque, N. M. 87102. (505) 842-3292.

The U. S. FISH AND WILDLIFE SERVICE is pleased to support the Watchable Wildlife effort in furtherance of its mission to preserve, protect, and enhance fish and wildlife resources and their habitats for the use and enjoyment by the American public. U. S. Fish and Wildlife Service, Post Office Box 1306, Albuquerque, N. M. 87103. (505) 766-2321.

 The mission of the BUREAU OF RECLAMATION is to manage, develop, and protect water and related resources in an environmentally and economically sound manner. Reclamation operates the Colorado River to provide Arizonans with balanced benefits from this most important resource. Reclamation's construction accomplishments in Arizona include the Central Arizona Project (CAP). CAP environmental investigations and habitat preservation projects assure that species such as the bald eagle and desert bighorn are able to maintain viable populations in Arizona. Bureau of Reclamation, Post Office Box 61470, Boulder City, NV 89006-1470. (702) 293-8420.

 The ARIZONA DEPARTMENT OF TRANSPORTATION serves the public as the key agency to plan, develop, maintain, and operate a high quality multi-modal transportation system. Through its magazine *Arizona Highways*, ADOT also publishes the official state highway map in addition to this premier monthly magazine with world-wide distribution. Statewide operations also provide licensing, registration and related revenue collection services through the Motor Vehicles Division. ADOT, 206 S. 17th Ave., Phoenix, AZ 85007. (602) 255-7357.

 THE NATIONAL FISH AND WILDLIFE FOUNDATION, chartered by Congress to stimulate private giving to conservation, is an independent not-for-profit organization. Using federally funded challenge grants, it forges partnerships between the public and private sectors to conserve the nation's fish, wildlife, and plants. National Fish and Wildlife Foundation, Bender Building, Suite 900, 1120 Connecticut Ave., N.W. Washington, DC 20036. (202) 857-0166.

 ARIZONA PUBLIC SERVICE COMPANY is Arizona's largest investor-owned electric utility serving all or part of 11 of the state's 15 counties. About 1.6 million people, or about 45 percent of Arizona's population, receive their electric service from APS. APS is committed to a clean, safe and healthy environment. We will, therefore, conduct all aspects of our business in an environmentally sensitive and economical manner. We believe these actions will not only benefit our customers, shareholders, employees and the communities we serve, but will also improve the quality of the environment in which we all live. Arizona Public Service Company, Post Office Box 53999, Phoenix, AZ 85072-3999.

OTHER IMPORTANT CONTRIBUTORS
The Nature Conservancy
Arizona Chapter of The Wildlife Society
Salt River Project

Welcome to Arizona!

Arizona is probably better known for its wonderful and varied scenery—the Grand Canyon, Sedona's Red Rock Country, Superstition Mountains, and Sonoran Desert. Arizona's citizens and visitors alike can take the opportunity to view many types of wildlife in these magnificent settings.

Take a minute to pause and discover not just the visual beauty of Arizona's settings, but the different creatures that live in and about these breathtaking scenes. From "birding" in the Huachuca Mountains, to deer on the Kaibab, waterfowl along the Colorado River, and many stops along the way, wildlife viewing will compliment your picture of Arizona.

Arizona is a state rich in fish and wildlife resources. There are over 800 different vertebrate species found in Arizona. Twenty-two species of amphibians, at least eighty-five different fish species, ninety-four reptiles, 136 mammals, and nearly 500 bird species have been recorded here. This diversity is a result of the varied landscapes and climatic patterns within our state.

State and federal wildlife and land management agencies and private organizations have joined to produce this *Arizona Wildlife Viewing Guide*. The *Guide* identifies ninety marked sites to help you enjoy and learn about our wildlife.

Arizona's total picture provides a breathtaking background with interesting and varied wildlife living in these special areas. Use this guide to experience the best of Arizona!

Enjoy Arizona, we do!

Fife Symington
GOVERNOR

OUTDOOR ETHICS

Honor the rights of private landowners. Gain permission of private landowners before entering their property.

Honor the rights of others to enjoy their viewing experience. Loud noises, quick movements, or erratic behavior that might scare wildlife is inappropriate. Wait your turn or seek another viewing opportunity.

Honor your own right to enjoy the outdoors in the future. Leave wildlife habitat in better condition than you found it. Pick up litter that you encounter and dispose of it properly.

INTRODUCTION

Some people who have never been to Arizona, and even some people who live here, believe the state offers little more than desert, cactus, and the Grand Canyon. True, a great deal of Arizona is desert, and there are lots of cacti, from the tiny pincushion to the giant saguaro. The majesty of the Grand Canyon is unforgettable. But Arizona is much more than desert land. There are rugged mountains, rolling, grass-covered hills, mountain meadows, and alpine tundra above 12,000 feet. There are places in the Kaibab Plateau and White Mountains that receive eight feet of snow annually. It is not unusual for Arizona to record both the daily high and low temperatures for the contiguous United States.

This diversified landscape has produced a varied mixture of habitats and large numbers of wildlife species. The native vertebrate fauna in Arizona include 829 species. When the introduced species are added, the total is nearly 900. Why so many? It is because of the complex patterns of vegetation, climatic conditions, and Arizona's unique location—near the coastal waters of the Gulf of California, the southern end of the Rocky Mountains, and the northern end of the Mexican Sierra Madre Mountains. Climatic conditions are further influenced by the sub-tropics to the south and the four North American deserts.

All of the above factors combine to give Arizona tremendous biological diversity, or *biodiversity*, a term used by wildlife experts to describe the natural abundance of plants and animals. Forty-three species of lizards and forty-nine species of snakes are found here, including seventeen distinct subspecies of rattlesnake. Dry though it is, Arizona is home to some eighty-five species of fish, sixty-one of which have been introduced in the last 100 years. The roster of mammals includes twenty-eight species of bats, and twenty-two carnivores, such as mountain lion, kit fox, and the elusive ringtail. Arizona is internationally-known as a birders paradise, with 475 native species, 268 of which nest here regularly.

Wildlife viewing opportunities in Arizona's scenic country are limited only by the length of your trip. Do take take time to pause, look, and listen—you'll be amazed at what can be seen!

THE NATIONAL WATCHABLE WILDLIFE PROGRAM

Wildlife management in Arizona traditionally has been directed at game species and hunting and fishing programs. Funding for these management activities has come from hunting and fishing license fees and from federal taxes on firearms and fishing equipment. Non-game wildlife has benefited from these sportsman-directed activities through habitat enhancement, law enforcement, research, acquisition of critical areas, and education programs.

In recent years, public interest in wildlife has increased significantly, due in part to environmental concerns and to the educational efforts of wildlife agencies and organizations. This interest has stimulated a change in direction for many wildlife agencies, including the development of watchable wildlife programs.

In 1970 the Arizona Game and Fish Department became one of the first state wildlife agencies to employ a full-time, non-game biologist, the beginning of a watchable wildlife program. A few years later Arizona initiated a non-game income tax checkoff to help fund these new wildlife programs. In 1990, Arizona voters passed the Arizona Heritage Initiative. This program will take twenty million dollars annually from lottery funds and allocate these dollars to protect sensitive wildlife habitat, environmental education, and historic preservation and parks. This guide is funded in part from Heritage dollars.

The *Arizona Wildlife Viewing Guide* is part of a national response to interest in wildlife viewing and the need to develop new support for wildlife programs. As part of The National Watchable Wildlife Program coordinated by Defenders of Wildlife, state and federal government agencies and private organizations in Arizona joined forces and funds to promote wildlife viewing, conservation, and education. This guide represents an important first step in this effort.

Selecting the viewing sites for this Guide was not an easy task. Arizona's wide variety of habitats support many different kinds of wildlife with many potential viewing areas. Over 180 sites were nominated by agency staff and others with wildlife interests. Sites were chosen by the steering committee to represent a cross-section of the state. About 130 candidate sites were visited by the author and ninety were selected. Sometimes it was possible to combine several sites into a vehicle route. The managing agency approved each selected site as a Watchable Wildlife area.

Site enhancement of individual viewing sites is the next step. This will involve such things as interpretive signs, trail development, viewing blinds or platforms and provisions for parking and restrooms. Some sites in this guide are already developed as Watchable Wildlife areas, while others have access as the only feature.

The National Watchable Wildlife Program is founded on the notion that the surest means to create support for wildlife is to first capture the heart. To view wildlife in a natural setting—a sunset flight of sandhill cranes, a family of desert bighorn sheep—is to feel awe, excitement, wonder. These experiences become the foundation upon which each of us builds an appreciation for and understanding of the natural systems and diversity of wildlife that surround us. From here, a person need take only the shortest of steps to feel genuine concern for our natural heritage, and its continued protection into the future.

VIEWING HINTS

The wildlife viewing sites in this guide include areas where wildlife may easily be seen, and other places where it may be more difficult. Some sites have interpretive trails with signs that point out where wildlife may be seen—other sites, however, may be a part of a mountain range, with no trails, no interpretive information, and no facilities. Wildlife watchers should take into account their outdoor experience, knowledge of wildlife, and amount of time available when selecting sites to visit.

Much of the excitement of wildlife viewing stems from the fact that you can never be sure what you may see. Although some days are better than others, there are several things you can do to greatly increase your odds of seeing wildlife:

Choose your season. Some of Arizona's wildlife can be seen only at certain times of the year. Sandhill cranes, for instance, may always be seen at Willcox Playa in the winter, but never during the summer. Many birds migrate north or south at certain times of year. Some mammals hibernate during the winter; others may remain hidden during the heat of a summer day.

Visit in the early morning and late evening. There is generally more wildlife activity in the first and last hours of daylight than at any other time of day. The low-angle sunlight of morning and evening also provides warm, rich colors that make beautiful photographs.

Use binoculars. A good pair of binoculars or a spotting scope will open up a whole new world of wildlife viewing. With a twenty power spotting scope, for example, it's possible to watch a desert bighorn sheep standing 1.5 miles away.

Come prepared. Many wildlife viewing sites in Arizona are remote and have no facilities. ALWAYS CARRY WATER, EVEN IN THE WINTER. Whether it is in mountains or the middle of the desert, dress appropriately for the site you plan to visit. Be sure to bring an Arizona road map; local USFS or BLM maps are also very helpful and will add to your viewing success.

Move slowly and quietly. There is probably nothing you can do to better improve your chances of seeing wildlife than to slow down. Allow for periods of silence before moving again. Animals often disappear as you arrive, but may return shortly if you are quiet enough. Use your ears to locate birds.

Use field guides. Field guides can tell you what habitats an animal prefers, when it is active, what it eats, and much more. Guides are available for nearly every kind of plant and animal found in Arizona.

Enjoy wildlife at a distance. Refrain from touching, feeding, or moving too close to animals. More often than not, young animals that appear to be orphaned have parents waiting in the shadows. If you believe an animal is injured, sick, or abandoned, contact the nearest wildlife agency.

Some wildlife is dangerous. Arizona is home to rattlesnakes, mountain lions, and black bears. Be aware that in certain areas these animals could be nearby, and maintain a safe distance if you encounter them.

Wildlife viewing requires patience. Spend enough time in the field. If you arrive at a site expecting to see all the species listed in this guide during one visit, you will likely be disappointed.

HOW TO USE THIS GUIDE

This Guide is arranged to coincide with the five travel regions of the state. Each site description includes the featured wildlife and the habitat in which each species may be seen. Additional information relating to viewing probability, viewing season and specific directions to the site is also provided. NOTES OF PRECAUTION RELATING TO ROAD CONDITIONS, SAFETY, VIEWING LIMITATIONS, AND LAND OWNERSHIP RESTRICTIONS ARE NOTED IN CAPITAL LETTERS. Each site description also displays symbols for featured wildlife, available facilities, site owner/management initials, plus a telephone number where additional site information may be obtained. Each viewing site will be marked by the binoculars logo, symbolic of the wildlife viewing sites across the nation. Arizona's area code is (602).

IMPORTANT NOTE: Highway numbers are subject to change–please supplement the directions in this guide with an up-to-date Arizona highway map.

SITE OWNER/MANAGER ABBREVIATIONS

USFS	U.S. Forest Service
BLM	Bureau of Land Management
AGFD	Arizona Game and Fish Department
USFWS	U.S. Fish and Wildlife Service
USBR	U.S. Bureau of Reclamation
NPS	National Park Service
ADOT	Arizona Department of Transportation
ASP	Arizona State Parks
ASLD	Arizona State Land Department
TNC	The Nature Conservancy

FEATURED WILDLIFE

Songbirds/ Perching Birds   Upland Birds   Waterfowl   Wading Birds   Shorebirds   Birds of Prey   Insects

Small Mammals   Hoofed Mammals   Carnivores   Freshwater Mammals   Fish   Reptiles & Amphibians   Wildflowers

FACILITIES AND RECREATION

Parking   Restrooms   Picnic Tables   Trails   Handicapped Accessible   Boat Ramp   Restaurant   Camping

Lodging   Fee   All Seasons   Spring   Summer   Fall   Winter

A R I Z O N A
Wildlife Viewing Areas

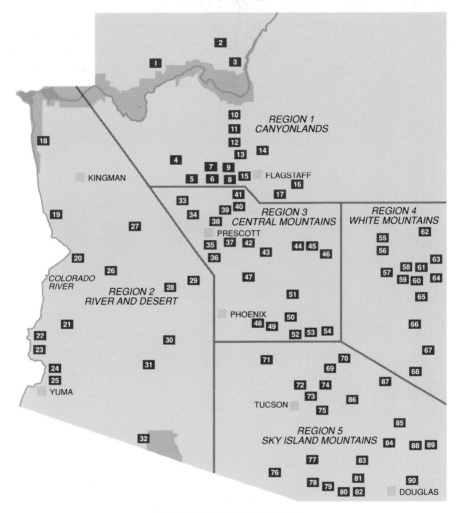

MAP INFORMATION

Arizona is divided into five bioregions relating loosely to geographical boundaries and habitat type. These five regions form the chapters of this guide. Viewing sites are numbered consecutively and follow a general pattern in each region.

1 This symbol indicates the location and number of a wildlife viewing site.

HIGHWAY SIGNS

As you travel across Arizona, look for these special highway signs that identify wildlife viewing sites. Most sites will have the binoculars logo to mark the viewing area or beginning of a route.

13

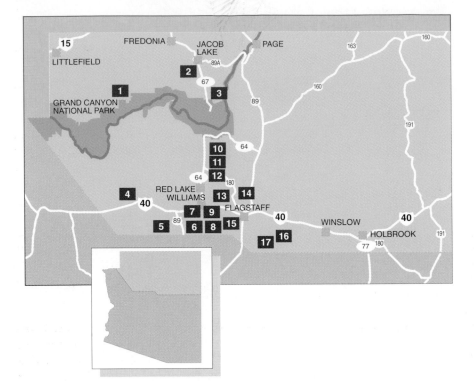

WILDLIFE VIEWING SITES

1 Mt. Trumbull

2 North Rim - Kaibab Plateau Parkway

3 House Rock Buffalo Ranch

4 Aubrey Valley

5 Big Black Mesa

6 Wagon Tire Flat

7 Coleman Lake

8 White Horse Lake - Pine Flat Route

9 Sunflower Flat

10 Grandview - 302 Road Loop

11 Red Butte

12 Red Mountain Geologic Area

13 Kendrick Park

14 Lamar Haines Memorial Wildlife Area

15 Rogers Lake

16 Raymond Buffalo Ranch

17 Mormon Lake - Doug Morrison Overlook

MOUNT TRUMBULL

Description: Located in one of the most isolated areas in Arizona, this site is fifty miles on a dirt road from the nearest town and there are no homes, farms or ranches along the way. The roads to Mount Trumbull cross miles of open land, home to a few pronghorn. The lower elevations of Mount Trumbull are pinyon pine and juniper. At the higher elevations are old-growth stands of Ponderosa pine and aspen. Mule deer are common in the pinyon-juniper habitat, but are hard to see in the dense vegetation. Wild turkeys and Kaibab squirrels are in the pine areas around Nixon Springs. Birds of the area include northern flicker, ash-throated flycatcher, Steller's jay, western bluebird, and the chipping sparrow.

Viewing Information: The best time to see wild turkeys is in the spring. Kaibab squirrels are easily seen except in winter. The Nixon Springs area has water but no recreation facilities. There is a trail to the top of 8,000-foot Mount Trumbull, the highest point for miles. ROADS CAN BE MUDDY WHEN WET, SNOW CLOSES ACCESS IN WINTER.

Directions: *From Fredonia, take Arizona 389 west for eight miles to the Mount. Trumbull Recreation Area turnoff. Follow signs along the fifty-mile-long road. There are two other routes to Mount Trumbull, from Colorado City and St. George, Utah. All go through scenic country, but the access from Fredonia is the best all-weather road.*

Ownership: BLM (801-628-4491)
Size: 16,000 acres   **Nearest Town:** Fredonia

The Merriam turkey is found in the Ponderosa pine forest in Arizona's mountains. The flocks, including young birds, are best seen in the fall. Look and listen in spring for the gobbling tom turkeys as they strut in hopes of attracting a hen.
LARRY R. DITTO

15

2 NORTH RIM-KAIBAB PLATEAU PARKWAY

Description: Starting at Jacob Lake, this route passes through Ponderosa pine, mountain meadows, and spruce-fir. The North Kaibab is famous for large-antlered mule deer. The history of deer management dates from 1906, when President Theodore Roosevelt created the Grand Canyon National Game Preserve. The Kaibab Plateau extends for forty-five miles east to west and sixty miles north to south, ending abruptly at the North Rim of the Grand Canyon. It is an excellent place to see mule deer and Kaibab squirrels. The black-bellied tassel-eared Kaibab squirrel is only found here and on Mount Trumbull in the Ponderosa pine. Goshawks, wild turkey, blue grouse, Williamson's sapsuckers, Clark's nutcrackers, red crossbills, and Grace's warbler are just a few of the birds at this site.

Viewing Information: There is a high probability of seeing mule deer in this high summer range, especially near the park entrance and along the edge of meadows. Kaibab squirrel are easy to see and are common in the Jacob Lake area. There are many forest roads in the area that offer excellent viewing opportunities and a greater chance to see wildlife. Arizona 67 is closed at Jacob Lake from November 15 to May 15.

Directions: From the junction of Arizona 67 and U.S. 89A at Jacob Lake, go south forty-four miles to the North Rim of the Grand Canyon. The park entrance is approximately twenty-six miles from Jacob Lake.

Ownership: ADOT, (255-7357);
USFS, (643-7395)
Size: Forty-four miles
Closest Town: Fredonia

Mule deer live in most areas of Arizona, from the Sonoran Desert to the spruce-fir forests. The North Kaibab is one of the most popular deer hunting areas in the state and supports between 10,000 and 15,000 mule deer.
BOB MILES

HOUSE ROCK BUFFALO RANCH

Description: House Rock Valley is along the eastern edge of the Kaibab Plateau and west of Marble Canyon and features a mix of shortgrass prairie, pinyon pine, and juniper trees. House Rock Buffalo Ranch is at the southern end of the valley. Bison are not native to Arizona and were brought to this area in 1905 as a private venture. State management of the herd began in 1927. There are about 125 bison roaming freely on the 65,000-acre ranch. Herd numbers are managed by annual fall hunts. Many mule deer come off the Kaibab plateau to winter here. Pronghorn are in the valley.

Viewing Information: The twenty-two-mile gravel road is open all year long. AVOID ROAD WHEN WET. Bison are not always near the main road, but there are several roads providing access to other areas of the bison ranch. DO NOT APPROACH BISON ON FOOT. Stay in vehicle. Pronghorn are sometimes seen along the main road. The best time to see mule deer is from December to March.

Directions: From Marble Canyon, go west on U.S. 89A for sixteen miles to the House Rock Buffalo Ranch road (Forest Road 455). Turn south and continue for twenty-two miles.

Ownership: USFS; AGFD (774-5046)
Size: 65,000 acres   **Closest Town:** Marble Canyon

Bison are not native to Arizona. Two state-managed herds of bison at House Rock Valley and Raymond Ranch offer an opportunity to see these animals of the Great Plains. A large bull bison can weigh over 2,000 pounds. BOB MILES

4 AUBREY VALLEY

Description: This broad, open grassland valley rimmed with the 1,000-foot-high Aubrey Cliffs to the east is home to hundreds of prairie dog towns and many pronghorn. Raptors such as golden eagles, red-tailed and ferruginous hawks cruise the valley skys. The black-footed ferret formerly occupied the area and plans are underway for their reintroduction. Most of the land along the highway is privately-owned. There are no facilities.

Viewing Information: Wildlife can be seen all year long—but the best time is from April to October. There is a high probability of viewing prairie dogs from the highway. Prairie dog towns begin about six miles west of Seligman.

Directions: From Seligman, take Historic Route 66 west for twenty-two miles. The viewing area ends at Mile Post 117.

Ownership: ADOT (255-7357)
Size: Twenty-two miles   **Closest Town:** Seligman

5 BIG BLACK MESA

Description: This twenty-one-mile vehicle route on Forest Road 573 travels through typical pinyon pine-juniper woodland. Mule deer, javelina, coyotes, pinyon jays, and raptors can be seen. Pronghorn frequent the open grassland at the northern end of the route.

Viewing Information: Best times for seeing wildlife is early morning or late evening in the spring and summer. The road follows the old Peavine Railroad grade along Limestone Canyon which provides some elevation for better viewing. An old limestone kiln is passed along the way. Roads can be muddy; AVOID WHEN WET.

Directions: From Paulden, go north on Arizona 89 for seven miles to Mile Post 344; turn west on Forest Road 573 (Bullock Road) and continue for twenty-one miles, returning to Arizona 89 two miles south of Ashfork.

Ownership: USFS (636-2302)
Size: Twenty-one-mile route
Closest Town: Paulden from south; Ashfork from north

6 WAGON TIRE FLAT

Description: This open grassland area is surrounded by pinyon pine and juniper woodlands. Pronghorn, mule deer, American kestrel, red-tailed hawks, and golden eagles may be seen here.

Viewing Information: Go past the flagstone quarry loading zone at the railroad and into the open grassland. Forest Road 492 goes to Grindstone and on to Perkinsville. Forest Road 186 goes to the northeast. Drive down any road in the area, but stay in the grassland to see pronghorn. Mule deer are usually in the woodlands and are harder to see. ROADS SHOULD BE AVOIDED WHEN WET. No facilities in this area.

Directions: From Paulden, go north on Arizona 89 for 9.6 miles to the Drake-Perkinsville Road. Turn east for about three miles. From Ashfork, go south on Arizona 89 for sixteen miles to reach the Drake-Perkinsville Road.

Ownership: USFS (636-2302)
Size: 6,000 acres
Closest Town: Paulden, from south; Ashfork, from north

7 COLEMAN LAKE

Description: In the Ponderosa pine forest, this small lake and wetland recently underwent habitat improvement to create islands and deeper water channels. Many water bird species are present, especially ducks, belted kingfishers, and killdeer. Elk, mule deer, and wild turkeys are common around the lake, and bald eagles winter here.

Viewing Information: This site sounds like a wildlife haven in spring, with birds calling and frogs croaking. Elk and mule deer are frequently seen in the spring and summer around the edge of the lake. The road is usually closed by snow from January through March. AVOID THE ROAD WHEN MUDDY. Fall colors can be outstanding.

Directions: From Williams, take Forest Road 173 (Perkinsville Road) south for 7.5 miles to Forest Road l08. Turn west for two miles to Coleman Lake.

Ownership: USFS (635-2633)
Size: Fifty acres   **Closest Town:** Williams

8 WHITE HORSE LAKE - PINE FLAT ROUTE

Description: This fifty-mile loop through Ponderosa pine and oak habitat has several viewing stops and two lakes where wildlife can be seen. White Horse Lake is a popular recreation area with all facilities. J.D. Lake, a small fly fishing lake, has only parking and is less crowded. There are many mule deer and elk in the area, which receives heavy use by hunters in the fall. Wild turkeys are also common. Waterfowl, cormorants, bald eagles, and osprey are seen at the lakes.

Viewing Information: In spring and summer, elk and mule deer are usually seen along this route, especially in the open meadow at Pine Flat. Bald eagles and osprey are common in winter and spring around both lakes. Spring is the best time to view wild turkeys. Plan on four hours to complete the loop. The road to White Horse Lake is open all year but the rest of the loop may close with winter snows. ROADS CAN BE MUDDY WHEN WET.

Directions: *From Williams, take Forest Road 173 (Perkinsville Road) south for nine miles. Turn east on Forest Road 110 and continue for 7.7 miles to White Horse Lake Road (Forest Road 109). To continue the loop, return to Forest Road 110 and go four miles, following the signs to J.D. Lake, located just beyond the junction with Forest Road 105. Continue on for eight miles to Pine Flat. There the road becomes Forest Road 354; continue straight ahead. Seven miles from Pine Flat is the paved Forest Road l73 (Perkinsville Road). Return to Williams.*

Ownership: USFS (635-2633)
Size: Fifty-mile route
Closest Town: Williams

The acorn woodpecker spends most of the year storing acorns in holes drilled in trees. In summer, however, this bird will feed on insects. Look for acorn woodpeckers in Ponderosa pine forest where Gambel oak trees are present.
DEDE GILMAN

Description: The Arizona Game and Fish Department, The Nature Conservancy, and the Kaibab National Forest have worked together to acquire this unique wetland in the Ponderosa pine forest. In wet years there may be 100 acres of water; in dry times it may be only a mud flat. Mallards, pintails, teal, cormorants, and other waterfowl are present in fall and spring. Elk, mule deer, and pronghorn are frequently present.

Viewing Information: To see elk or deer, walk the last .5-mile using binoculars to view the opposite shoreline. Wintering bald eagles and other raptors will roost in nearby pine snags. Waterfowl are present in large numbers in fall and spring. Walking the shoreline will provide the best viewing opportunities. WINTER SNOWS WILL CLOSE ROAD. ALSO AVOID WHEN WET.

Directions: *From Williams, take Forest Road 173 (Perkinsville Road) south and follow the signs to White Horse Lake. Just before entering the White Horse Lake campground, turn left on Forest Road 109 and go 1.9 miles to Forest Road 14. Travel 1.1 mile on Forest Road 14, then look for a two-track, unmarked road to the left. Sunflower Flat is about .5-mile down this road.*

Ownership: AGFD; USFS (635-2633)
Size: 160 acres   **Closest Town:** Williams

The native Merriam elk of Arizona were extinct by about the turn of the century. The elk seen in Arizona today are descendants of Rocky Mountain elk brought here in the 1920s from Yellowstone National Park. Elk are common in the forested areas along the Mogollon Rim from Williams to Alpine. BUDDY MAYS

10 GRANDVIEW-302 ROAD LOOP

Description: This route passes through Ponderosa pine and some pinyon pine-juniper woodland adjacent to Grand Canyon National Park. The area has good populations of mule deer, elk, and wild turkey. Abert squirrels are common. The area is fairly good for songbirds, including hairy woodpecker, northern flicker, western flycatcher, mountain chickadee, and pigmy nuthatch. A few miles past the Grandview Lookout is a section of the route with some very old, twisted juniper trees.

Viewing Information: This forty-five-mile gravel road is passable to all types of vehicles in good weather. THE ROAD CAN BE MUDDY, AVOID WHEN WET. Winter snows will close this road. The Arizona Trail, for hikers and horsemen, goes the length of Arizona. At Grandview Lookout a section of this trail has interpretive information. There is a high probability of seeing mule deer, elk, wild turkeys, and Abert squirrels. This is a popular big game hunting area in the fall. There are no recreational facilities along the route.

Directions: *From Arizona 64 at Tusayan, take Forest Road 302 east for sixteen miles to Grandview Lookout. (This section of the loop has the best road conditions). From Grandview Lookout, turn right onto Forest Road 310 for about seven miles to Forest Road 311, turn right, and continue for four miles to Forest Road 320. Turn right again and go .2-mile to Forest Road 301. At this point, you may either continue seventeen miles on Forest Road 320 to reach Arizona 64, twelve miles south of Tusayan; or you can turn right on Forest Road 301 for eighteen miles to Forest Road 302 and Tusayan.*

Ownership: USFS (638-2443)
Size: Forty-five miles   **Closest Town:** Tusayan

Most animals hear much better than humans. Why? The outer ears of many animals are much larger than ours, and more directional. You can test this by simply cupping your hands around your ears—notice how your hearing improves.

11 RED BUTTE

Description: This volcanic butte rises abruptly from the surrounding pinyon pine-juniper area to an elevation of 7,370 feet and is visible from Arizona 64. This is a restricted roadless area, although a forest road encircles the butte. Elk, mule deer, coyotes, and jackrabbits are common. The bluffs povide nesting habitat for red-tailed hawks, prairie falcons, golden eagles, and ravens.

Viewing Information: A mile-long trail to the top of Red Butte provides an excellent vista and a good opportunity to see wildlife. There is a moderate probability of seeing elk, mule deer, pronghorn, and coyotes, especially in spring and early fall. Golden eagles are not frequently seen. The road to the trailhead and around Red Butte can be muddy. AVOID WHEN WET.

Directions: From Tusayan, go south on Arizona 64 for about eleven miles to Forest Road 320. Turn east and go one mile to Forest Road 340. Turn north, go .9 mile and turn right on Forest Road 340A for .3 mile to the trailhead.

Ownership: USFS (638-2443)
Size: 2,500 acres **Closest Town:** Tusayan

Coyotes occur in all areas of Arizona. They hunt small animals, mostly at night. Their high-pitched yapping is a common sound in the evening and early morning.
STEVE PRIDGEON

12 RED MOUNTAIN GEOLOGIC AREA

Description: This is an interesting volcanic site, with steep cliffs that provide nesting habitat for raptors and ravens. It is in pinyon pine-juniper woodland with large Ponderosa pine trees in the narrow canyon leading to the cliff area. Steep hills of loose volcanic cinders add to the scenic value. Golden eagles and prairie falcons nest here. Elk and mule deer are in the wooded area, while Abert squirrels inhabit the Ponderosa pine.

Viewing Information: A well-marked trail, less than a mile long, connects the parking area to the cliffs. DO NOT ATTEMPT TO CLIMB CLIFFS; VIEW NESTING RAPTORS FROM A DISTANCE. Elk may be seen where the canyon begins to narrow—approach slowly and quietly for the best chance to see them. In May, June, and July the probability of seeing nesting raptors is high. The road to the parking area can be muddy, AVOID WHEN WET.

Directions: *From Flagstaff, go north on U.S.180 for thirty-one miles to the Red Mountain Geologic Area turnoff. It is .4 mile to the parking area.*

Ownership: USFS (526-0866)
Size: 1,225 acres   **Closest Town:** Flagstaff

13 KENDRICK PARK

Description: This large, open mountain meadow is bisected by U.S. 180 and surrounded by Ponderosa pine, spruce-fir forests, and patches of aspen. It is an excellent area to see pronghorn and elk. Fall colors can be outstanding, and the view of the San Francisco Peaks is breathtaking.

Viewing Information: There is a Forest Service picnic area on the north side of Kendrick Park and a small parking area on the south end. The highway through the meadow does not have safe places to park. There are forest roads around Kendrick Park. Respect the private property in the area. Early morning and late evening hours are the best times to look for pronghorn in the meadow and elk around the edges and along the highway. Winter snows sometimes close the road.

Directions: *From Flagstaff, go north on U.S. 180 for twenty-one miles to Kendrick Park.*

Ownership: USFS (526-0866)
Size: 2,000 acres   **Closest Town:** Flagstaff

Description: This old homestead on the south slope of the San Francisco Peaks has two springs in a small scenic mountain meadow surrounded by large boulders. A small creek and pond are formed by the spring water. There are many large Ponderosa pine and fir trees mixed with aspen. This is an excellent site for songbirds of the mixed-conifer habitat, including Lewis, downy, hairy and three-toed woodpeckers; also western flycatchers, mountain chickadee, red-breasted and white-breasted nuthatches, and brown creepers. Elk, mule deer, and Abert and red squirrels are found here as well.

Viewing Information: The old road to the homestead provides easy access and good visibility to this walk-in viewing area. This trail starts at the gate and goes to the right. A walk to the homestead takes about forty-five minutes. Another trail goes straight, following a narrow meadow into the National Forest. There is an excellent chance to see cavity-nesting birds. Go early and move quietly for a good chance to see elk and mule deer. Winter snows will close access to this area.

Directions: *From Flagstaff, go northwest on U.S. 180 for seven miles to the Snowbowl Road (Forest Road 516). Turn north and go 4.5 miles to the small parking area at the Wildlife Area entrance.*

Ownership: AGFD (774-5045)
Size: 160 acres   **Closest Town:** Flagstaff

A quiet and secluded site in the mixed conifer forest on the San Francisco Peaks, Lamar Haines Memorial Wildlife Area is an excellent area to look for many forest birds. JOHN N. CARR

25

15 ROGERS LAKE

Description: This large intermittent lake at 7,200 feet is surrounded by Ponderosa pine forest. In wet years there are several hundred acres of shallow water. An excellent area to see large numbers of elk. During wet years, waterfowl can be present in fall and spring.

Viewing Information: August and September are the best times to see elk and mule deer from the main road. Winter snows can result in road closures. There is an unmaintained road around Rogers Lake for additional access, but AVOID WHEN WET.

Directions: From Flagstaff, at the corner of Milton Road and Historic Route 66, take Route 66 west for two miles to Woody Mountain Road. Turn south and proceed six miles to Rogers Lake.

Ownership: ASLD; USFS (526-0866)
Size: 1,000 acres   **Closest Town:** Flagstaff

16 RAYMOND BUFFALO RANCH

Description: Located in open grassland and pinyon pine-juniper habitat, this site is managed to maintain a herd of eighty-five free-roaming bison. It is also home for pronghorn and winter range for elk.

Viewing Information: Bison are wild animals and can be dangerous; DO NOT APPROACH. Bring binoculars and stay on the roads. Pronghorn can be seen from the main road into the ranch. Elk arrive during the cold winter months and stay in remote areas. Please call prior to visiting this site—bison may not be near the main roads. The ten-mile graded road to the Ranch can be very treacherous when wet or snow-covered.

Directions: From Flagstaff, go east on Interstate 40 for twenty-seven miles to Exit 225. Proceed south on this dirt road for ten miles to the ranch headquarters.

Ownership: AGFD (774-5045)
Size: 15,000 acres   **Closest Town:** Flagstaff

September and early October are the best times to hear bull elk bugling in the forested areas of northern Arizona. Spring is the best time to hear the mating rituals of blue grouse, which make a rapid thumping sound on hollow logs or stumps. Early morning or late evening are the best times to look and listen for these wildlife spectacles.

Description: The largest natural lake in Arizona, Mormon Lake can be little more than a mud flat in very dry years. At 7,300 feet, it offers a mix of habitats, including wetlands, open water, grassland, coniferous forest, and cliffs. Migratory waterfowl by the hundreds are common. Wintering bald eagles, osprey, and peregrine falcons may be seen. Elk, mule deer, and pronghorn also occur here.

Viewing Information: There is a paved road around Mormon Lake. The best viewing site is at the Doug Morrison Overlook on the east side. Here, above the cliffs, is an outstanding view of the lake and the San Francisco Peaks, the highest in Arizona at 12,000 feet. Waterfowl are best seen in March and April and September through November. Rock wrens occur around the cliffs, while horned larks, coyotes, and pronghorn are in the grasslands. This is an excellent site for wintering bald eagles from November through April. Winter storms may cause temporary road closures.

Directions: *From Flagstaff, on Interstate 17 at Exit 339, take Lake Mary Road (Forest Highway 3) southeast for twenty-one miles to Mormon Lake. Forest Road 90 circles around the west side of the lake to recreational facilities and returns to Forest Highway 3.*

Ownership: USFS (556-7474)
Size: Nine square miles
Closest Town: Flagstaff

About thirty pairs of "southwestern" bald eagles nest in cliffs and large trees along rivers and lakes in the desert of central Arizona. During the fall migration, Mormon Lake is one of the best sites to see some of the 250 northern bald eagles that winter near Arizona waters.
STEVE PRIDGEON

27

WILDLIFE VIEWING SITES

18 Willow Beach, Lake Mead National Recreation Area

19 Topock Marsh-Havasu National Wildlife Refuge

20 Bill Williams Delta National Wildlife Refuge

21 Kofa National Wildlife Refuge

22 Cibola National Wildlife Refuge

23 Imperial National Wildlife Refuge

24 Mittry Lake Wildlife Area

25 Betty's Kitchen

26 Alamo Lake State Park

27 Burro Creek Campground

28 Hassayampa River Preserve

29 Castle Hot Springs Road

30 Robbins Butte Wildlife Area

31 Painted Rocks

32 Quitobaquito Spring/Organ Pipe Cactus National Monument

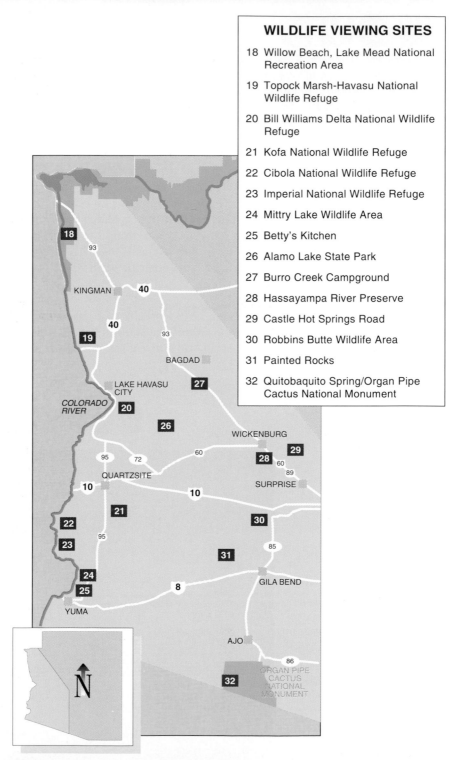

18 WILLOW BEACH, LAKE MEAD NAT. REC. AREA

Description: In the upper reach of Lake Mohave on the Colorado River, this site maintains a significant population of desert bighorn sheep. Willow Beach has a National Fish Hatchery that rears trout and is open to the public. Desert tortoise are also found here, though not frequently seen.

Viewing Information: From a boat there is a high probability of seeing bighorn sheep in the early morning hours of the hot summer months. Go either up or downstream for about ten miles. Bighorn sheep visit the river to drink or feed on vegetation at the water's edge. Boat rentals are available.

Directions: From Kingman, take U.S. 93 north for fifty-eight miles to the Willow Beach turnoff. From Boulder City, Nevada, take U.S. 93 south for fourteen miles. Willow Beach is four miles from U.S. 93.

Ownership: NPS (702-293-8906);
Willow Beach Resort (767-3311)
Size: Twenty miles

19 TOPOCK MARSH-HAVASU N. W. R.

Description: Topock Marsh is a remnant of the original marshlands along the Colorado River. USBR and USFWS cooperate in water management to maintain this habitat. The open water, cattail stands, old tree snags, and adjacent desert combine to attract a wide variety of birds. White pelicans, double-crested cormorants, egrets, black-crowned night herons, western grebes, sandpipers, and kingfishers are commonly seen. In winter there are many ducks, Canada and snow geese. Gambel's quail are common along the shore. Bald eagles, osprey, and marsh and red-tailed hawks are also found here.

Viewing Information: U.S. 95 along the east side of the marsh provides four viewing access points. Boat rentals are available and provide the best viewing opportunities. Viewing is excellent all year and in winter for migrating waterfowl, with a moderate probability of seeing bald eagles and osprey in winter. Refuge headquarters is located in Needles, California.

Directions: From Interstate 40 at Exit 1, just east of the Colorado River bridge, go north on U.S. 95 toward Bullhead City. The access point mileages from Interstate 40: South Dike, two miles; Catfish Paradise, 2.5 miles; Five Mile Landing, 4.4 miles and North Dike, eight miles.

Ownership: USFWS (619-326-3853)
Size: 3,800 acres   **Closest Town:** Needles, California

20 BILL WILLIAMS DELTA NATIONAL WILDLIFE REFUGE

Description: The Bill Williams River enters Lake Havasu, forming marsh habitat and an outstanding riparian forest of cottonwood, willow, and salt cedar. The road along the river travels between the riparian habitat and the black volcanic bluffs of the Buckskin Mountains, home to desert bighorn sheep. Many birds are found in the area with migratory waterfowl common in the winter. Waterbirds include western and Clark's grebes, kingfishers, double-crested cormorants, and egrets. Among the songbirds found are Costa's hummingbirds, ash-throated flycatchers, hooded and northern orioles. Small mammals include the roundtail and Harris antelope ground squirrels, raccoons, badgers, and jackrabbits. Common reptiles here include chuckwalla, and spiny, whiptail and collared lizards. Rattlesnakes are common in the warmer months.

Viewing Information: In winter there is an excellent chance to see many kinds of migratory birds. Early morning and late evening provide the best chance to see bighorn sheep, especially with binoculars. Reptiles are highly visible in the warmer months. The ten miles of graded gravel road to the eastern Refuge boundary can be rough at times, but the road is passable for all types of vehicles. ROAD MAY BE FLOODED AT TIMES; USE CAUTION. The parking area north of the bridge on U.S. 95 provides a good viewing point. The only recreational facilities in the area are along the Colorado River.

Directions: *From Parker, go north on U.S. 95 for eighteen miles to the Refuge Road, turn east and go ten miles. The Refuge Road is just south of the bridge.*

Ownership: USFWS (667-4144)
Size: 6,105 acres   **Closest Town:** Parker

The black-tailed rattlesnake has a distinctive dark snout and charcoal black tail. This yellowish snake with dark blotches is usually about three feet long. They are not very aggressive and may not rattle when disturbed. All rattlesnakes are dangerous and should be avoided. RANDALL D. BABB

21 KOFA NATIONAL WILDLIFE REFUGE

Description: Established in 1939, this refuge protects the 800 to 1,000 desert bighorn sheep that live in the very rugged Kofa and Castle Dome Mountains. Other wildlife include desert tortoise, mule deer, kit fox, white-winged doves, golden eagles, and red-tailed hawks. The Harris antelope ground squirrel is common. A checklist of 185 birds is available.

Viewing Information: Desert bighorn sheep in their native habitat are not easy to see. January and February are the best times to look—an early morning visit to popular Palm Canyon and Horse Tank offers the best chance to view these animals. Use binoculars or a spotting scope, and listen! Observation blinds are available to the public; check at headquarters. This is a wilderness area so access is limited to existing roads. Camping is permitted but facilities are not available. Visitors are advised to contact the Refuge headquarters in Yuma for maps, checklists, and before any lengthy visit. This area is extremely hot and dry in the summer months—please come prepared.

Directions: There are four marked entrances to the Refuge off U.S. 95 between Yuma and Quartzsite. These are the recommended roads as many others require four-wheel-drive vehicles.

Ownership: USFWS (783-7861)
Size: 660,000 acres   **Closest town:** Yuma

22 CIBOLA NATIONAL WILDLIFE REFUGE

Description: This refuge features a mixture of farming for wildlife, riparian habitat, and the Colorado River, a combination attractive to waterfowl. As many as 25,000 Canada geese winter here. The area draws sandhill cranes, snow geese, and ducks of many kinds. Egrets, herons and Gambel's quail are year-round residents. Brown pelicans and wood storks are seen occasionally.

Viewing Information: This is the best area in Arizona to see Canada geese. Take the Goose Loop Road, a self-guided vehicle route of 2.5 miles. This route is open weekdays from 10am to 3pm in the winter.

Directions: From Interstate 10 on the west side of Blythe, California, take the Neighbors Boulevard exit and travel south for seventeen miles (across the Colorado River) to the refuge.

Ownership: USFWS (857-3253)
Size: 16,267 acres
Closest Town: Blythe, California

RIPARIAN HABITAT

In Arizona, riparian habitats comprise only one percent of the land area. Yet these narrow, fertile strips along streams and canyon bottoms harbor the greatest diversity of plants and animals of any habitat type. Riparian habitats are easily disrupted, and as a result only a small percent of these pristine areas remain.

This habitat, dependent upon adequate moisture from streams or springs, is very visible in Arizona since most of the surrounding area is dry upland desert. The classic cottonwood-willow riparian forests are evident along the Verde River in central Arizona and the San Pedro River in the southeast. At higher elevations, sycamores, alder, ash, Arizona walnut, canyon grape, and poison ivy can also be present.

Riparian habitats are not just cottonwood-willow or sycamore communities: they may take the form of a drier mesquite bosque (forest), a wet marsh, or a line of vegetation extending down a canyon bottom due to the cooler, wet conditions not found in the surrounding area. Arroyos—dry streams and channels—support more and larger plants that are common in adjacent areas. These "dry riparian" habitats are created from the extra moisture provided by runoff from seasonal rains, creating a haven for many insects, birds, and

Riparian habitat along the San Pedro River near Fairbank.
RANDY A. PRENTICE

mammals. The largest paloverde and ironwood trees of the Sonoran Desert are found near these arroyos.

Many wildlife species are largely or totally dependant on the riparian deciduous forest. The Arizona gray squirrel, Apache fox squirrel, and raccoon are examples. Bats roost in riparian trees and feed upon the great number of insects produced there. Many bird species depend on riparian habitats. At the San Pedro River National Conservation Area, for example, 350 bird species have been identified, three-fourths of those recorded in Arizona. These riparian habitats provide the necessary requirements for bald eagles, gray hawks, yellow-billed cuckoos, great blue herons, Mississippi kites, and many other birds.

After a drive through the Bill Williams Delta National Wildlife Refuge, look at the surrounding hills: the difference in vegetation is remarkable and demonstrates how important this riparian habitat is to the wildlife of Arizona. To see wildlife in Arizona, go to the riparian areas—the animals do!

Riparian vegetation supports large numbers of insects, including the rainbow grasshopper. Insects are an essential food source for many birds during the nesting season.
ALEX KERSTITCH

23 IMPERIAL NATIONAL WILDLIFE REFUGE

Description: This refuge extends thirty miles along the Colorado River and was established in l941 to protect the desert and river ecosystems. The marsh-river habitat here is surrounded by some of the driest and hottest desert in the west, and shows the sharp contrast between river and desert. Along the river are ducks and Canada geese in winter, as well as egrets, herons, sandpipers, and pelicans. In the desert, look for Gambel's quail, Gila woodpeckers, black phoebes, and nighthawks. Desert mammals include desert bighorn sheep, mule deer, kit foxes, wild horses, and burros.

Viewing Information: A viewing platform at the headquarters offers a good view of the wildlife agricultural fields and the Colorado River. The Red Cloud Mine Road to the north has four turnouts that overlook the river. The Painted Desert Trail, 2.8 miles north of the headquarters, is a one mile self-guided interpretive trail through some very interesting desert. There are rattlesnakes in this area—please use caution. In winter there is a high probability of seeing many kinds of birds. The headquarters, open 7:30 am to 3:30 pm weekdays, has interpretive information and a natural history exhibit. A bird checklist is available.

Directions: *Approximately twenty-three miles north of Yuma on U.S. 95 turn west on Martinez Lake Road. Follow the signs for thirteen miles to refuge headquarters.*

Ownership: USFWS (783-3371)
Size: 25,765 acres
Closest Town: Martinez Lake

The marshes, mudflats, and waters of the Colorado River attract thousands of birds at Imperial National Wildlife Refuge. JACK W. DYKINGA

Description: Mittry Lake is a 400-acre oxbow of the Colorado River. It has well-developed wetland and marsh with bulrush and cattails adjacent to some very harsh and barren desert. Open water channels have been dredged to create edge effect habitat for wildlife. Many cottonwood trees have been planted on the dry sites in an attempt to re-establish riparian habitat. This is an area cooperatively managed by the AGFD, BLM, and USBR. Although extremely difficult to see, the endangered Yuma clapper rail is fairly common here. Pied-billed grebes, great blue herons, egrets, and a variety of ducks are common at this site. Mittry Lake is excellent for canoeing or small motorized boats.

Viewing Information: The access road along the Gila Gravity Canal is elevated and provides an excellent view of the marsh. The winter migration period, November to February, provides the best viewing opportunity—up to 10,000 waterfowl can be present. Early morning hours are best for viewing. Beavers inhabit the area but are rarely seen because they dig holes in the bank rather than building the more common twig-and-branch dams and lodges. Camping is allowed, but there are no recreational facilities.

Directions: From Yuma, go east seven miles on U.S. 95, turn north onto Avenue 7E (Laguna Dam Road). Follow this road ten miles past Laguna Dam and Betty's Kitchen to the Mittry Lake Wildlife Area. Road access is along the Gila Gravity Canal.

Ownership: USBR; BLM, (726-6300); AGFD, (342-0091)
Size: 3,575 acres
Closest Town: Yuma

Marbled godwits are fairly common in winter along the Colorado River. They are large shorebirds, sixteen to twenty inches in length, and have a long slightly upturned bill. PHILLIP ROULLARD

25 BETTY'S KITCHEN

Description: This wildlife interpretive area is along the Colorado River and just upstream from Laguna Dam. Heavy vegetation attracts waterfowl, herons, egrets, and many songbirds. The site is just south of Mittry Lake.

Viewing Information: The .5-mile trail winds through tunnels of vegetation with interpretive stops along the way. Water birds are common in winter and spring. Commonly seen birds include phainopepla, Abert's towhee, green-backed heron, egrets, Harris' hawk, and Wilson's, yellow-rumped and orange-crowned warblers.

Directions: From Yuma, go seven miles east on U.S. 95 to Avenue 7E (Laguna Dam Road). Turn north and follow this road for nine miles to just past Laguna Dam. Turn left and follow the sign to Betty's Kitchen.

Ownership: BLM (726-6300)
Size: Ten acres   **Closest Town:** Yuma

26 ALAMO LAKE STATE PARK

Description: This is a remote but popular park near a large reservoir. The habitat is in a transition area between the Sonoran and Mohave Deserts. The lake attracts large numbers of waterfowl in the winter and other water birds such as egrets, great blue herons, cormorants, white pelicans, and occasionally brown pelicans. The upper end of the lake is a developing riparian area of cottonwoods and salt cedar, and shelters white-wing and mourning doves. Redwing and yellow-headed black birds are frequently seen in the upper lake area. Mule deer and desert bighorn sheep are present but rarely seen, and there are many wild burros here. A bald eagle nest site is in the upper part of the lake. Interesting Joshua trees, large tree-like yucca, are east of the lake.

Viewing Information: This is a nice, fully developed recreational park with a visitor center. Winter months are best for viewing water birds. There is a high probability of seeing wild burros, especially in summer when they are attracted to the water. The bald eagle nesting site is protected and closed in spring.

Directions: From Wenden, take Alamo Road north for thirty-eight miles.

Ownership: ASP (669-2088)
Size: 5,600 acres
(lake 2,500 to 3,000 acres)
Closest Town: Wenden

27 BURRO CREEK CAMPGROUND

Description: This nice campground is located in a deep canyon in an area between the Sonoran and Mohave Deserts. Flowing water in Burro Creek creates riparian habitat, attracting great blue herons, mergansers, mallards, teal, and other waterfowl. Golden and bald eagles as well as black- and zone-tailed hawks frequent this area. Swallows and swifts are along the cliffs. Long fin dace, a small native fish, are in the creek, with red-spotted toads along the banks. Whiptail and zebra-tailed lizards are common in the warm months, as are diamondback rattlesnakes—please be careful.

Viewing Information: Near the campground entrance is an informative cactus garden. High probability of seeing waterfowl and hawks fall through spring. In summer, early morning and late evening are the best times to see reptiles and other wildlife.

Directions: *Burro Creek Campground is fifty-eight miles north of Wickenburg and fifteen miles south of Wikieup on U.S. 93.*

Ownership: BLM (757-3161)
Size: 120 acres   **Closest Town:** Wikieup

28 HASSAYAMPA RIVER PRESERVE

Description: In the floodplain of the Hassayampa River, this site has a riparian woodland of cottonwoods, willows, and large mesquites. Four-acre Palm Lake attracts great blue herons, snowy egrets, and ducks, and is a refuge for five species of native desert fish. The bird checklist of 229 species includes some rare Arizona hawks; zone-tailed and sharp-shinned hawks, and Mississippi kites. Mule deer, javelina, raccoons, and ringtails frequent the riparian area. Zebratail and whiptail lizards are common.

Viewing Information: The preserve is open Wednesday through Sunday, with winter hours from 8 am to 5 pm and summer hours from 6 am to noon. Interpretive information is available at the visitor center and bookstore. There are guided walks and self-guided trails. Desert wildlife is attracted to the riparian areas, especially in the dry summer months. The Gilbert skink, a rare Arizona lizard, lives in the woody debris. On Monday or Tuesday, visit the state highway roadside rest area two miles to the south.

Directions: *The preserve is three miles south of Wickenburg on U.S. 60.*

Ownership: TNC (684-2772)
Size: 340 acres   **Closest Town:** Wickenburg

29 CASTLE HOT SPRINGS ROAD

Description: This route is a thirty-six-mile gravel road through typical Sonoran Desert habitat in the Hieroglyphic Mountains. It passes Lake Pleasant, a large irrigation storage reservoir with many recreational developments, including an interpretive center. Typical desert wildlife seen along this route include Harris antelope ground squirrels, jackrabbits, Gambel's quail, Gila woodpecker, cactus wren, phainopeplas, and Harris' and Cooper's hawks. Mule deer and javelina frequent the area.

Viewing Information: January is the best time to see mule deer and javelina. A greater variety of birds can be seen in winter and spring. Golden eagles are occasionally seen near the historic Castle Hot Springs Resort. This is a narrow and winding mountain road and for three miles follows the creek bottom—this road may be closed in the rainy seasons. The Lake Pleasant interpretive center offers information about desert wildlife. There is private property along this route; please respect it. There are no facilities.

Directions: From Phoenix, take Interstate 17 north to Exit 223 (Arizona 74-Lake Pleasant Road). Turn west for twelve miles to Castle Hot Springs Road, turn north and continue until it returns to Arizona 74. The road to the Lake Pleasant Visitors Center is two miles before the Castle Hot Springs Road turnoff.

Ownership: ASLD, BLM (863-4464)
Size: Thirty-six miles   **Closest Town:** Phoenix

The javelina or peccary is a native of the southwest. Their reputation for being dangerous is greatly exaggerated. Javelina weigh less than fifty pounds and have a scent gland on their back that is used to keep herds together. The average herd size is eight to ten animals. BOB MILES

Description: Located on the south side of the Gila River, this wildlife area is managed by AGFD for small game, primarily mourning and white-winged doves. The area has farm fields planted in grain crops with dense mesquite thickets along the north boundary. In the summer, thousands of doves nest in the mesquite trees and feed in the fields. Many Gambel's quail can be seen. Cottonwood and mesquite trees have been planted to enhance the riparian habitat. The area is also home to many raptors, mostly harriers. The annual Christmas bird count here has averaged sixty-five species. The area has Gila monsters and abundant rattlesnakes in the summer—please be careful.

Viewing Information: An early morning or late evening in August is the best time to view the thousands of feeding doves. September first is the opening day of dove hunting season. Winter is the best time to see hawks and songbirds. Half a mile south of the Robbins Butte Wildlife Area entrance is the Fred Weiler Greenbelt Overlook which provides an excellent view of the entire area.

Directions: *From Phoenix, go west on Interstate 10 about thirty miles. At Exit 112 (Arizona 85), go south eight miles (past the town of Buckeye) to the entrance. The dirt road into the wildlife area extends for two miles.*

Ownership: AGFD (981-9400)
Size: 1,440 acres   **Closest Town:** Buckeye

Thousands of white-winged doves arrive in southern Arizona starting in mid-April. They build nests in mesquite and salt cedar thickets, and return to Mexico by mid-September. The saguaro cactus fruit, shown here, is an important part of the birds' diet. C. ALLAN MORGAN

PAINTED ROCKS

Description: In addition to its wildlife, this site includes a small mound of black rocks with hundreds of prehistoric Native American pictures, called petroglyphs, cut into the stone. This is a great place to see many lizard species native to Arizona. Looking down from the tops of the rocks are the chuck-walla and desert spiny lizards. Fast-moving zebra-tail and leopard lizards will be on the desert floor. Also in the area are Gila monsters, desert iguanas, and whiptail lizards. Commonly seen birds include the cactus wren, Gila wood-pecker, harrier, red-tailed hawk, and turkey vulture.

Viewing Information: Desert lizards are best viewed when temperatures are moderate, in March and April or October and November. Mid-summer temperatures at this site can be in excess of 115 degrees, and even lizards seek shade in this heat! There are recreational facilities here, but no water, so bring plenty.

Directions: From Gila Bend, go west on Interstate 8 for thirteen miles to Exit 102. Turn north on Painted Rocks Road for eleven miles to the Petroglyph Unit.

Ownership: BLM (863-4464)
Size: Twenty acres   **Closest Town:** Gila Bend

One of Arizona's largest lizards, the chuckwalla can reach eighteen inches in length. They eat the buds, flowers, and leaves of desert plants. When disturbed, the chuckwalla will hide in rock cracks and crevices and gulp air, inflating itself so that it can't be pulled out. BOB MILES

Description: This site is a true oasis in the vast Sonoran Desert, a rarity in Arizona. It is located only a few hundred yards from the International border in Organ Pipe Cactus National Monument, about halfway around the Puerto Blanco Drive. The spring and small pond are home for an endangered subspecies of desert pupfish. The oasis attracts many birds, including vermillion flycatchers, coots, phainopepla, and killdeer.

Viewing Information: You must stop at the Visitor Center prior to going to Quitobaquito Spring. Excellent interpretive information about the flora and fauna of the monument is available. Complete recreational facilities are near the visitor center. At Quitobaquito Spring there is a short trail from the parking area to the spring. The small pupfish, just over an inch long, is easily seen, especially in the spring breeding season when the males turn bright blue and become very active. While summer temperatures often exceed 100 degrees, the rest of the year is moderate.

Directions: From Ajo, proceed east ten miles on Arizona 86 to Why. Turn south on Arizona 85 for twenty-two miles to the Visitor Center and directions to Puerto Blanco Drive and Quitobaquito Spring.

Ownership: NPS (387-6849)
Size: 330,000 acres (spring size ten acres)
Closest Town: Ajo

Organ pipe cactus are found in the Organ Pipe Cactus National Monument and nearby areas. This variety of cactus has large, lavendar-white flowers that open only at night in May, June, and July. LAURENCE PARENT

REGION 3 - CENTRAL MOUNTAINS

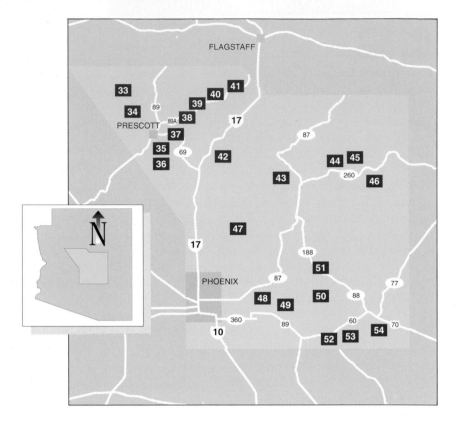

WILDLIFE VIEWING SITES

33 Camp Wood Route

34 Fair Oak Tonto Road Loop

35 Lynx Lake

36 Cedar Tank Wildlife Habitat Project

37 Prescott Valley Antelope Drive

38 Mingus Mountain Campground

39 Dead Horse Ranch State Park -
    Tavasci Marsh

40 Page Springs Fish Hatchery

41 Red Rock State Park

42 Beasley Flat Recreation Site

43 Tonto Natural Bridge State Park

44 Tonto Creek Recreation Area

45 Rim Recreation Area/Forest
    Road 300

46 Canyon Creek

47 Verde River - Horseshoe Dam

48 Phon D. Sutton Recreation Area

49 Lost Dutchman State Park

50 Fish Creek

51 Roosevelt Lake Wildlife Area

52 Boyce Thompson Southwestern
    Arboretum

53 Oak Flat Recreation Area

54 Pinal Mountains - Signal Peak

33 CAMP WOOD ROUTE

Description: Beginning in the open grassland at about 5,000 feet, this route into the Santa Maria Mountains passes through chaparral, juniper woodland, and Ponderosa pine. A large, open mountain meadow, unusual habitat for this area, is found at Yolo Ranch. Depending upon the habitat, pronghorn, mule deer, elk, wild turkeys, and numerous songbirds may be seen. Camp Wood is a Forest Service summer work station in the pines.

Viewing Information: Pronghorn are common in the open grassland, while elk and deer are more likely to be seen in the Yolo Ranch meadow during summer. Yolo Ranch is private property, please respect it. Wild turkeys can be seen in the pines in April and May. Steller's and pinyon jays are common. It is a twenty-two-mile drive to Yolo Ranch; the road then continues for another thirty miles to Bagdad. It will take at least four hours to drive this thirty-mile stretch! THIS IS A VERY ROUGH, ROCKY ROAD; A HIGH-CLEARANCE VEHICLE IS ESSENTIAL. Forest Road 21 can become very muddy when wet and should be avoided. NO FACILITIES ALONG ROUTE.

Directions: From Prescott, drive twenty-two miles north on the Williamson Valley Road (to the end of the pavement), then turn west onto Forest Road 21. It is sixteen miles to Camp Wood and twenty-two miles to the Yolo Ranch meadow. At this point, all but the most adventuresome should turn around and return to Prescott.

Ownership: USFS (445-7253)
Size: Twenty-two miles one-way
Closest Town: Prescott

In spring and summer, the summer tanager may be found in the wooded areas of central and southeastern Arizona, and sometimes along Colorado River riparian areas. It rarely winters in Arizona.
BRYAN MUNN

34 FAIR OAK—TONTO ROAD LOOP

Description: This loop tour through private and Prescott National Forest lands traverses juniper-pinyon pine, oak woodland, chaparral, and open grassland habitats. Pinyon jays, red-tailed hawks, American kestrels, and Gambel's quail are common. In the wooded habitats are mule deer and javelina, with pronghorn in the grasslands.

Viewing Information: January is the best time to see mule deer. Javelina are common but seldom seen. Pronghorn are frequently seen all year on the northern part of this route. Fair Oak and Tonto Roads are graded dirt roads; AVOID WHEN WET. No facilities along route.

Directions: *In northwest Prescott, take Iron Springs Road west for about twelve miles to Tonto Road (Forest Road 102). Turn north, staying on Forest Road 102 for seventeen miles, then turn right onto Fair Oak Road (Forest Road 85). Travel 2.5 miles before turning south onto Williamson Valley Road for the twenty-mile return trip to Prescott.*

Ownership: Pvt.; USFS (445-7253)
Size: Forty-nine miles   **Closest Town:** Prescott

35 LYNX LAKE

Description: Located in the Bradshaw Mountains south of Prescott, this popular recreation area has a mix of Ponderosa pine, oak woodland, and riparian habitat. Around much of the shoreline of this 55-acre lake is a narrow band of marsh habitat that draws red-winged blackbirds and marsh wrens. The water also attracts great blue herons. Bald eagles and waterfowl winter here and osprey are frequently seen in spring. There is a nice riparian area along a creek between the boat ramp area and the upper campground.

Viewing Information: There is a high probability of seeing waterfowl and eagles in winter, and herons all year. Excellent birding during the spring migration period. Explore the riparian area for warblers and flycatchers. Trails around the lake provide easy access. Campgrounds are closed in winter.

Directions: *From Prescott, go east on Arizona 69 for four miles to Walker Road. Turn south for three miles to the Lynx Lake Recreation Area. There are four entrances, two for day use areas and two for campgrounds.*

Ownership: USFS (445-7253)
Size: 200 acres
Closest Town: Prescott

Description: This is a pond area, fenced to enhance vegetation at the water's edge, in brushy chaparral habitat at the base of the Bradshaw Mountains. Mule deer and javelina frequent the area. Mallards, pintails, teal and other waterfowl are on the pond in winter.

Viewing Information: Best viewing here is in the early morning and late evening. Scan the area with binoculars from the road before walking to the pond. Waterfowl are often present in the winter months. During the hot dry months, mule deer and other wildlife will come to drink. Patience and quiet are needed here. No facilities at this site. Parking is available along the road on either side of the cattleguard. DURING WET WEATHER THE ROAD CAN BE EXTREMELY MUDDY AND SHOULD BE AVOIDED.

Directions: In Mayer, from Arizona 69 and Central Avenue, turn west. Follow Central Ave. for about .3 mile to Miami Street. Turn south to Main Street. Turn west on Main St. and go .2 of a mile to a three-way junction. Take Wicks Road to Jefferson and turn south on Forest Road 67 (the old Goodwin Road). (This sounds difficult but just head uphill toward the small church with a steeple.) Continue for four miles to Cedar Tank on the left. The .25 mile trail is along an old road bed.

Ownership: USFS (445-7253)
Size: Five acres   **Closest Town:** Mayer

Arriving as early as September, pintail ducks are among the first waterfowl to pass through Arizona on their long migration flights. Small ponds like Cedar Tank provide resting places for many species of waterfowl.
GRADY ALLEN

37 PRESCOTT VALLEY ANTELOPE DRIVE

Description: Pronghorn can be seen in the shortgrass prairie on both sides of this road. Kestrels are common and prairie falcons are seen frequently.

Viewing Information: Pronghorn are almost always seen along this eight-mile-stretch of graded road. Pronghorn fawns are born in late May and June and this is an excellent site to watch these frisky little runners. There are no facilities along this lightly-traveled road, and only a few pullout areas for parking. Most of the land adjacent to the road is private—viewing is restricted to the road. Don't forget binoculars. AVOID ROAD WHEN WET.

Directions: *From Prescott Valley, go southeast on Arizona 69 for three miles to Fain Road (County Road 179). Turn north and continue for the eight miles between Arizona 69 and U.S. 89A. At U.S. 89A turn around or turn west and go to Prescott.*

Ownership: Private; ASLD; Yavapai County (no phone available)
Size: Eight-mile route   **Closest Town:** Prescott Valley

38 MINGUS MOUNTAIN CAMPGROUND

Description: At 7,600 feet, this site is in a mountain meadow with Ponderosa pine. Mule deer, Merriam's turkey, Abert squirrels and band-tailed pigeons can be seen here.

Viewing Information: Best viewing times are early morning in summer and fall. A nature trail provides access for viewing. The road up Mingus Mountain goes through a variety of vegetative types and offers vistas of the Verde Valley. Traveling through the old mining town of Jerome is worth the trip. The campground is closed from December to March due to snow and poor road conditions.

Directions: *From Cottonwood, take U.S. 89A southwest through Jerome about sixteen miles to Forest Road 104. Continue on Forest Road 104 about three miles to the campground.*

Ownership: USFS (567-4121)
Size: Fifty acres
Closest Town: Jerome

DEAD HORSE RANCH STATE PARK - TAVASCI MARSH

Description: This state park is located along the Verde River and has some of the best examples of cottonwood-willow riparian forest in Arizona. The combination of desert, riparian habitat, and a flowing river offer a unique contrast of habitats. The area is home to over 100 species of birds. Gambel's quail, bald eagles, osprey, yellow-billed cuckoos, prairie falcons, belted kingfishers, and many species of waterfowl have been seen here. The riparian area supports raccoons and other small mammals. Seven species of bats have been recorded. The park also has a small Quetta pine seed orchard. North of the park entrance 1.5 miles is Tavasci Marsh, a twenty-acre wetland with active beaver dams that attracts all kinds of waterfowl and shorebirds.

Viewing Information: Many trails in the park and along the Verde River offer a good chance to see riparian-associated wildlife. Tavasci Marsh is a new wildlife area with limited facilities, but with a high probability of seeing marsh birds and beavers. The state park offers a fully-developed campground.

Directions: In Cottonwood, get on Main Street, then turn north on 5th Street, crossing the Verde River to the park entrance. Tavasci Marsh can be accessed from the park by continuing past the entrance for 1.5 miles. From the north go behind the Tuzigoot National Monument and down the hill for a mile.

Ownership: AGFD; ASP (634-5283)
Size: 600 acres
Closest Town: Cottonwood

The great blue heron is a large wading bird, about four feet tall and with a six-foot wingspan. It is frequently seen standing quietly in shallow water hunting for a meal of fish or frogs. BUDDY MAYS

40 PAGE SPRINGS FISH HATCHERY

Description: Page Springs Fish Hatchery has recently undergone extensive renovation. This new facility was designed to produce 1.2 million catchable-size rainbow trout per year. It is an impressive place, with a spring that produces fifteen million gallons of water per day, modern trout production facilities, a visitor center, and riparian habitat along Oak Creek. Many birds are seen here, including Lucy's and yellow-rumped warblers, hooded and Bullock's orioles, and black and rough-legged hawks. Page Springs is also home to some endemic snails.

Viewing Information: The visitor center has many interpretive exhibits, and the nearby wildlife watching area and nature trail are all designed to inform visitors about trout production and the wildlife of the area. Handicap access is provided to the hatchery.

Directions: *From Interstate 17, take Exit 293 (McGuireville) and go west toward Cornville for seven miles. At Casey's Corner turn north onto Page Springs Road and go four miles to the hatchery entrance.*

Ownership: AGFD (634-4805)

Size: 150 acres   **Closest Town:** Cornville

41 RED ROCK STATE PARK

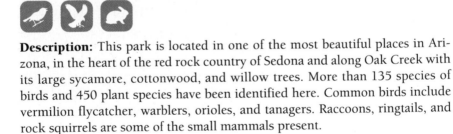

Description: This park is located in one of the most beautiful places in Arizona, in the heart of the red rock country of Sedona and along Oak Creek with its large sycamore, cottonwood, and willow trees. More than 135 species of birds and 450 plant species have been identified here. Common birds include vermilion flycatcher, warblers, orioles, and tanagers. Raccoons, ringtails, and rock squirrels are some of the small mammals present.

Viewing Information: Bald eagles are seen in winter; black hawks nest here in spring. Raccoons and ringtail cats are nocturnal and difficult to see. Use the well-marked trail system to look for wildlife. All developments have been built to suit the surrounding environment and include interpretive trails and an environmental education center.

Directions: *From Sedona, go three miles west on U.S. 89A and turn onto Lower Red Rock Loop Road for two miles to the park entrance.*

Ownership: ASP (282-6907)

Size: 286 acres   **Closest Town:** Sedona

42 BEASLEY FLAT RECREATION SITE

Description: This is a newly-developed recreation site along the Verde River. Geologic conditions here have left the river essentially void of riparian vegetation. The trees are primarily scrubby mesquites, while both up and downstream large riparian cottonwood trees are dominant. Desert cottontail rabbits, blacktail jackrabbits, badgers, and ringtails are present. Birds seen here include roadrunners, summer tanagers, cliff swallows, great blue herons, Gambel's quail, phainopepla, and belted kingfishers. Downstream is a southern bald eagle nesting site which is protected during nesting season. Across the river are prehistoric Indian ruins carved into the cliffs.

Viewing Information: Nature trails with interpretive information follow the Verde River. Wildlife can be seen all year, but spring is the best time. This area is a launching site for rafting down the Verde River.

Directions: *From Interstate 17 take Exit 287 (Arizona 260) for three miles through Camp Verde. At Salt Mine Road (Forest Road 574), turn west and continue eight miles to Forest Road 529. Turn east and drive two miles to Beasley Flat.*

Ownership: USFS (567-4121)
Size: Six acres   **Closest Town:** Camp Verde

The black-tailed jackrabbit is common in open areas and is most active in the early morning and evening. In summer, look for these animals resting in the shade of small trees or bushes. TOM & PAT LEESON

43 TONTO NATURAL BRIDGE STATE PARK

Description: The natural travertine bridge across Pine Canyon is 150 feet wide and arches 185 feet over the creek below. Spring water falling from the top of the arch creates an unusually moist habitat for wildlife. The arch under the bridge and well-developed riparian area along Pine Creek provide habitat for water dippers, canyon wrens, Bell's vireo, downy woodpeckers, ash-throated flycatchers, and mountain bluebirds. The canyon setting is also home for rock squirrels, raccoons, and the nocturnal ringtail. White-tail and mule deer inhabit the surrounding area but are not commonly seen.

Viewing Information: An outstanding area for wildlife viewing as well as geological and historical interests. The visitor center is on the National Register of Historic Places. There is a steep trail to the creek, the best place for viewing. Spring and summer are the best times to see birds. THE ROAD INTO THE PARK IS STEEP, TRAILERS ARE NOT PERMITTED. Space for trailer parking is provided 1.5 miles from the park.

Directions: *From Payson, go north on Arizona 87 for twelve miles to the park entrance road, turn west and continue for three miles.*

Ownership: ASP (476-4202)
Size: 160 acres
Closest Town: Payson

Formed by deposits of limestone, Tonto Natural Bridge is the world's largest natural travertine bridge. The misty, moist canyon creates a unique and lush habitat for many species of birds, animals, reptiles, and plants. PATRICK FISCHER

44 TONTO CREEK RECREATION AREA

Description: A very popular summer recreation area located just under the Mogollon Rim. Canyon habitat consists of cottonwood, willow, Arizona walnut, and Rocky Mountain maple. The surrounding area is Ponderosa pine with Gambel oak. A wide variety of songbirds are attracted to this area, including American dipper, yellow-rumped warbler, and acorn woodpecker. Rufous, black-chinned and broad-tailed hummingbirds are common in spring and summer. Mammals include elk, mule deer, Abert and rock squirrels.

Viewing Information: There are several trails providing easy access to the forest. In 1990 the Dude Fire burned near here, consuming 24,000 acres. There are self-guided auto tours showing fire damage and recovery—contact the Payson Ranger District for details. The AGFD Tonto Fish Hatchery is at the end of the road and open to the public on weekdays 8:00 am to 4:00 pm. There is a very good chance to see elk, Abert squirrels and many songbirds.

Directions: From Payson, go east on Arizona 260 for seventeen miles to the Tonto Creek Recreation Area (Forest Road 289). Turn north and follow the creek four miles to the hatchery.

Ownership: USFS (474-7900)
Size: Four miles
Closest Town: Payson

45 RIM RECREATION AREA - FOREST ROAD 300

Description: This scenic loop drive along the Mogollon Rim travels through mixed conifer, small stands of aspen, and small mountain meadows. Several small ponds are near the road, including Five Mile Lake near the junction of Forest Roads 34 and 75. Elk, mule deer, turkey and Abert squirrel are present.

Viewing Information: This route starts near Woods Canyon Lake, a very popular area featuring all recreational facilities. Along the Rim there is a handicapped-accessible trail which offers an outstanding view. From May through October there is an excellent chance to see elk and mule deer from the road.

Directions: From Payson, go east on Arizona 260 for thirty-one miles to Forest Road (FR) 300 and the Rim Recreation Area. Follow FR 300 six miles to FR34. Turn north and proceed three miles to FR 75. Continue on FR 75 for 5.5 miles until it returns to FR 34. Turn right on FR 34 and go to FR 300 and the starting point.

Ownership: USFS (289-2471)
Size: Twenty-seven miles   **Closest Town:** Payson

46 CANYON CREEK

Description: Just under the Mogollon Rim, Canyon Creek is a very scenic area of mountain meadows, riparian trees, and Ponderosa pine. Many birds are seen here, especially during the spring migration. Look for black-chinned, broad-tailed and rufous hummingbirds, spotted owls, red-naped sapsuckers, acorn woodpeckers, western bluebirds, and American dippers. Elk, mule deer, and wild turkey are also in the area.

Viewing Information: The upper canyon (on Forest Road 33) has no meadows, but open stands of Ponderosa pine. The AGFD Canyon Creek Trout Hatchery is open to the public weekdays from 8:00am to 4:00pm. The lower canyon (on Forest Road 188) has beautiful mountain meadows, but the road is a little rougher. There is a high probability of seeing all species, especially in May and June. Winter snows make these roads treacherous. AVOID ROADS WHEN WET.

Directions: *From Payson, go east on Arizona 260 for thirty-four miles to Young Road (Forest Road 512). Turn south and continue for three miles to Forest Road 33, turning east on Forest Road 33 for five miles to the upper canyon. To reach the lower canyon, return to the junction of Forest Roads 33 and 34. Take Forest Road 34 to Forest Road 188 past the Valentine Ridge Campground and continue one mile to the creek.*

Ownership: USFS (474-7900)
Size: 2,000 acres   **Closest Town:** Payson

A resident of old-growth forests and canyons, the Mexican spotted owl is difficult to see because it seldom moves. Once seen, however, the bird can be approached quite easily. Like all owls, it sleeps during the day and hunts silently at night for small mammals. BOB MILES

Description: The riparian habitat of the Verde River is bordered by the mountainous Sonoran Desert, carpeted in spring with yellow, blue, and purple wildflowers. The river has large cottonwood, sycamore, and willow trees, and the Mesquite Recreation Area is in a mature mesquite bosque. Many birds are attracted to the river, including cardinals, vermilion flycatchers, Bullock's oriole, verdins, black-tailed gnatcatchers, bald eagles, Harris', and red-tailed hawks. Great horned owls are heard at night and sometimes seen roosting in trees during the day. Great blue herons and egrets wade the river. Javelina and mule deer are present but not often seen. Reptiles here include whiptail, zebra-tail, spiny and tree lizards, Gila monsters, desert tortoise, and western diamondback and Mohave rattlesnakes.

Viewing Information: An excellent site for wildlife. Spring and fall are the best times for all species. Reptiles are not visible in winter, but many migrating birds stop by. Desert tortoise and Gila monsters are not common and are difficult to find. There are several access points to the river between the Mesquite Recreation Area and Horseshoe Dam.

Directions: From Carefree, go east on Cave Creek Road for six miles to Forest Road 205. Turn right and follow the signs eighteen miles to Horseshoe Dam.

Ownership: USFS (488-3441)
Size: Five miles   **Closest Town:** Carefree

The large, heavy-bodied Gila monster, the only venomous lizard in the United States, can reach twenty inches in length. The Gila monster's diet includes newborn small mammals, lizards, and bird eggs. These lizards are dangerous, but are slow and can easily be avoided. ALEX KERSTITCH

THE SONORAN DESERT

Arizona is the only state with all four North American deserts: the Chihuahuan, Mohave, Great Basin, and Sonoran. The Sonoran Desert is by far the most diverse in its vegetation and wildlife species. Located in the southwest quarter of Arizona, it is best known for the wide variety of cacti, including the giant saguaro seen in this background photo.

A wide variety of wildlife species and habitats are found here. Large mammals include desert bighorn sheep, mule deer, javelina, and even mountain lions and pronghorn. Endangered Sonoran pronghorn live in the extremely dry area of the Cabeza Prieta Wildlife Refuge, between Ajo and Yuma along the Mexican border. Many of the smaller mammals are nocturnal or live underground to avoid the heat of summer. The large-eared kit fox hunts kangaroo rats and other small animals at night. The round-tailed and Harris antelope ground squirrel are common and active during the day.

The many cactus species are important to desert wildlife. Javelina eat the prickly pear pads, spines and all. Cactus wrens, curved bill thrashers, and other birds nest in the protective cover of the cholla cactus. The Gila woodpecker and gilded flicker excavate holes for nesting cavities in the giant saguaro cactus; other birds, including the American kestrel,

Sonoran Desert viewed from Signal Hill, Saguaro National Park.
RANDALL K. ROBERTS

Lucy's warbler, elf and screech owls, purple martins, and phainopeplas all compete for the use of these nesting cavities. White-winged doves feed on the saguaro seeds. The red-tailed and Harris' hawks use the saguaros as hunting perches.

Snakes and lizards are probably the best known wildlife of the Sonoran Desert. The Gila monster, the only poisonous lizard in the U.S., is fairly common but rarely seen. Rattlesnakes are more common, more visable, and especially at the beginning of summer, more active. Lizards are easy to see and can be approached. The best time to view lizards is in spring as temperatures warm up. The large, slow chuckwalla and the small, quick zebra-tail lizard are two of many species found here.

There are several very good places to learn about the Sonoran Desert. The best are the Saguaro National Park near Tucson and the Organ Pipe Cactus National Monument near Ajo. The Arizona-Sonora Desert Museum near Tucson is an outstanding facility that interprets the relationships of these Sonoran Desert wildlife with their habitats.

The desert tortoise depends on cacti and other desert vegetation for food, including the fruit of the prickly pear cactus.
GEORGE H. H. HUEY

48 | PHON D. SUTTON RECREATION AREA

Description: This site is at the confluence of the Verde and Salt Rivers. Both rivers are controlled by upstream dams maintaining relatively large flows, unusual in this desert environment. This is one of the few places where bald eagles nest in the desert. (The nest sites are protected). Red-tailed and Harris' hawks, osprey, phainopepla, cactus wren, and Gambel's quail are common along the nature trail.

Viewing Information: The Lower Salt River Nature Trail loop begins at the northwest corner of the parking lot and passes through riparian and desert habitat. Best viewing times are late fall through early spring. If winter moisture is above average, wildflowers can be spectacular in March. Camping for self-contained trailers is available only in the winter. The Bush Highway provides access to several other recreational areas along the Salt River that are extremely popular in summer when thousands of young people come to go tubing.

Directions: From the junction of U.S. 60 and Powers Road in Mesa, go north on the Bush Highway for 9.5 miles to Phon D. Sutton Recreation Area turnoff, go north one mile to parking area. Access is also available from the junction of Bush Highway and Arizona 87 by driving south on the Bush Highway for about twelve miles to the Phon D. Sutton turnoff. This route will travel past Saguaro Lake.

Ownership: USFS (379-6446)
Size: 100 acres   **Closest Town:** Mesa

The confluence of the Verde and Salt Rivers in central Arizona is an excellent birding area, due to the flowing water and riparian habitat adjacent to Sonoran Desert vegetation. LES MANEVITZ

49 LOST DUTCHMAN STATE PARK

Description: This park in Sonoran Desert upland provides a scenic view of the Superstition Mountains, site of the legendary Lost Dutchman gold mine. The desert here is lush with paloverde and ironwood trees and giant saguaro cactus. Desert wildflowers can be spectacular after above average winter rains. Common birds are the Gila woodpecker, cactus wren, Gambel's quail, curve-billed thrasher, and Harris's and red-tailed hawks. Small mammals include round-tailed and Harris antelope ground squirrels, and desert cottontail. This area has many reptiles including Gila monsters and rattlesnakes.

Viewing Information: Many trails in the park lead into the Superstition Mountains. One trail near the park entrance is handicapped-accessible. In early morning these trails provide the best opportunity for viewing desert wildlife. Checklists of birds and plants are available.

Directions: *From Apache Junction go northeast on the Apache Trail (Arizona 88) for five miles to the park entrance.*

Ownership: ASP (982-4485) **Size:** 320 acres
Closest Town: Apache Junction

50 FISH CREEK

Description: The scenic Apache Trail to Fish Creek passes the Superstition Mountains and Canyon Lake on the Salt River. Fish Creek drains from the Superstition Mountains through a steep, narrow gorge, opening up for two miles. This riparian habitat with cottonwoods, willows, Arizona walnut, and ash trees is home to canyon wrens, cardinals, pyrrhuloxia, phainopeplas, and sulphur-bellied and vermilion flycatchers. Rock and Harris antelope ground squirrels are common. Mule deer, javelina, and bighorn sheep are in the mountains. The Gila chub is a small native fish in this stream.

Viewing Information: Winter and spring are the best times to see birds. Large mammals are difficult to see; early morning and evening are best—use binoculars. Except for the last few miles, the road to Fish Creek is paved. Fish Creek Hill is steep and narrow.

Directions: *From Apache Junction, go northeast on Arizona 88 (Apache Trail) for twenty-four miles to Fish Creek Bridge. Parking area is on the left, about .5 mile past the bridge.*

Ownership: USFS (379-6446)
Size: 200 acres **Closest Town:** Apache Junction

51 ROOSEVELT LAKE WILDLIFE AREA

Description: Roosevelt Dam was one of the West's first reclamation projects, creating a large reservoir in the Sonoran Desert. This water attracts large numbers of Canada and snow geese and other waterfowl in winter. The Tonto Creek arm of the lake is a refuge and some areas are closed to entry in winter to provide a safe resting area for geese. Bald eagles and osprey are also found here. Harris antelope ground squirrel, javelina, mule deer, and Gambel's quail inhabit the desert area. A well-developed cottonwood-willow riparian forest borders Tonto Creek just before it enters the lake near the A Cross road. Look in this area for yellow-billed cuckoos, hooded orioles, great blue herons, and black-crowned night herons.

Viewing Information: In winter there is a high probability of seeing hundreds of Canada geese along the lakeshore from Arizona 188. Tonto Basin Ranger District at Roosevelt has interpretive information and arrangements for guided bird walks can be made. Deer and javelina are fairly common and there is a good chance of seeing them, especially in areas along the Three Bar access road into the mountains. The Harris antelope ground squirrel is common and is active in the warmer months.

Directions: *From Roosevelt, go north on Arizona 188 along the Roosevelt Lake shore about twelve miles to the A Cross road. Several campgrounds serve as access points along the road.*

Ownership: AGFD, (981-9400); USFS, (467-3200)
Size: 22,550 acres
Closest Town: Roosevelt

The Harris antelope ground squirrel is common in the Sonoran Desert. This dimunitive animal runs with its tail curled above its body and is one of the few desert mammals active during the heat of the day. LAURENCE PARENT

52 BOYCE THOMPSON S.W. ARBORETUM

Description: An excellent place to learn about the vegetation of the Southwest. The arboretum's diverse plant life attracts an array of wildlife, including ninety species of butterflies. The 240 bird species include Costa's hummingbird, brown-crested flycatcher, cactus wren, ruby-crowned kinglet, and Gambel's quail. Other wildlife include the rock and Harris antelope ground squirrels, desert cottontail rabbits, collared and Arizona alligator lizards. The endangered desert pupfish and Gila topminnow, two native fish, are in Ayer Lake, on the east end of the arboretum.

Viewing Information: Viewing opportunities are available all year. Spring is the best time to see the small native fish. Early morning in mid March, the park and community celebrate the return of a flock of migrating turkey vultures. The visitor center has interpretive information, checklists for birds, butterflies, mammals, reptiles, and amphibians.

Directions: The arboretum is three miles west of Superior on U.S. 60.

Ownership: U of A; ASP (689-2723)
Size: Forty-five acres
Closest Town: Superior

53 OAK FLAT RECREATION AREA

Description: Nestled among large rocks is a small pond and marsh with cottonwood and willow trees. The surrounding habitat is Emory oak, manzanita and juniper. The water attracts waterfowl in winter. Many songbirds come to the riparian habitat including black-throated and gray warblers, verdins, plain titmouse, black-throated sparrows, and Bewick's and canyon wrens. White-tail deer and javelina occur in the wooded area but are difficult to see. Ringtails, racoons, and bobcats are present, but are nocturnal.

Viewing Information: Spring and summer are best for songbirds, with a high probability of seeing many species. Follow the paved road past two ponds. One pond and marsh are closest to the campground; the other pond is down in a nearby valley. At times traffic is heavy. Parking along the paved road is limited.

Directions: From Superior, drive east four miles on U.S. 60, through scenic Queen Creek Canyon, to the Oak Flat Recreation Area entrance on the right. The campground is .5 mile from the highway.

Ownership: USFS (425-7189)
Size: 200 acres   **Closest Town:** Superior

54 PINAL MOUNTAINS-SIGNAL PEAK

Description: The road in the Pinal Mountains to Signal Peak passes through chaparral, mountain riparian, and pine-fir forest habitat. Riparian habitat in Russell Gulch at the Sulphide Del Ray Campground is an excellent place to observe birds, especially hummingbirds. At the mountaintop are several communication towers that may be coated with millions of ladybugs in late May, June, and July. Painted red-starts and robins are two of many bird species found here. White-tail deer and javelina can be seen from the road. Abert squirrels are common in the pines.

Viewing Information: Mountaintop pines and fir create a beautiful setting for watching wildlife. High probability of seeing white-tail deer and Abert squirrels in spring and summer. Costa's and rufous hummingbirds are easily seen when spring wildflowers bloom. Several trails near the top of the mountain provide access to roadless areas. The winding gravel road is narrow but passable by all types of vehicles. The road can be muddy; AVOID WHEN WET. Winter snows can close the road.

Directions: *Between Globe and Miami at the junction of Arizona 88 and U.S. 60 turn south. Follow the signs to Pinal Mountain Recreation Area approximately sixteen miles.*

Ownership: USFS (425-7189)
Size: Sixteen miles
Closest Town: Miami

After emerging from their larval form in the valleys below and eating their fill of aphids, ladybugs converge by the millions on southern Arizona mountaintops in May and June. Here they will go through an estivation period, or summer hibernation.
LAURENCE PARENT

REGION 4 - WHITE MOUNTAINS

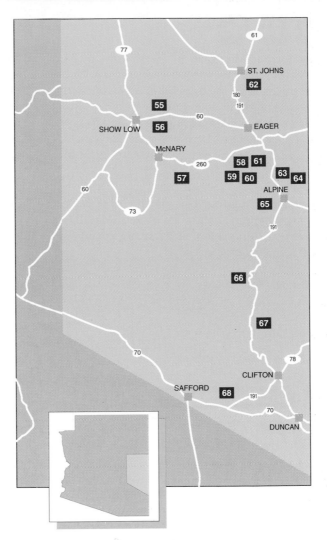

WILDLIFE VIEWING SITES

55 Allen Severson Memorial
   Wildlife Area

56 Jacques Marsh

57 Williams Creek National
   Fish Hatchery

58 Pole Knoll

59 Mount Baldy Trail

60 Lee Valley Lake

61 Springerville - Big Lake Loop

62 Lyman Lake State Park

63 Escudilla Mountain - Terry Flat

64 Luna Lake

65 Hannagan Loop

66 Eagle Creek - Honeymoon
   Campground

67 Coronado Trail

68 Bonita Creek

55 ALLEN SEVERSON MEMORIAL WILDLIFE AREA

Description: The town of Show Low, in cooperation with the Apache-Sitgreaves National Forest, became the first Arizona community to create artificial wetlands for the disposal of wastewater effluent. The marshes here actually treat and purify this wastewater; the result is an eye-pleasing, unoffensive wetland. Many birds are attracted to the 370-acre marsh surrounded by pinyon pine-juniper habitat. Common waterbirds include mallard, pintail, cinnamon teal, gadwall, yellow-headed blackbird, great blue heron, killdeer, and belted kingfisher.

Viewing Information: This marsh area is also called Pintail Lake as the highway signs indicate. Follow a well-defined trail to an observation platform with interpretive information. Birds are present all year and there is a high probability of seeing many species.

Directions: *From Show Low, go north on Arizona 77 for four miles. Turn east at the Pintail Lake sign and continue for .3 of a mile to the parking area.*

Ownership: USFS (368-5111)
Size: 370 acres   **Closest Town:** Show Low

56 JACQUES MARSH

Description: In 1978 the communities of Pinetop and Lakeside initiated construction of a marsh complex to treat wastewater effluent. Ninety-three acres of marsh with eighteen waterfowl nesting islands were created. Situated in a large, open meadow surrounded by pine forest, the marsh habitat not only attracts waterfowl but many elk—as many as 250 appear during the winter. Among the 1,500 waterfowl that have been observed in one day are mallard, pintail, redhead, canvasback, green-winged, blue-winged and cinnamon teal.

Viewing Information: The fenced area has no facilities. From the parking area go through the gate and walk the berms. Waterfowl are present all year as some nest here. High probability of seeing elk at sunrise and sunset in the cooler months.

Directions: *From Lakeside, just east of the USFS Ranger Station, take Porter Mountain Road for 1.5 miles to Juniper Drive. Turn left and continue for .6 mile to the parking area.*

Ownership: USFS (368-5111)
Size: 120 acres   **Closest Town:** Lakeside

Description: This hatchery rears the Apache trout, Arizona's only native trout, and raises trout for Indian reservations. The golden-colored Apache trout is native to the high mountain streams of Mt. Baldy. The hatchery is located in Ponderosa pine mixed with riparian and meadow-marsh habitat created by the large springs that supply the pristine water needed for rearing trout. Many species of wildlife occur here, including blue-throated, rufous and broad-tailed hummingbirds in spring. Bald eagles, osprey, goshawks, wild turkeys, American dippers, wood ducks, and Lewis and acorn woodpeckers are found in the vicinity. Black bear, elk, white-tail and mule deer are also here.

Viewing Information: Spring and summer are the best viewing times and there is a high probability of seeing many species. Bears frequently come to the hatchery area in spring but there is a low probability of seeing them; white-tail deer are also present but seldom seen. The eight-mile trip to the hatchery offers a good chance to see elk and mule deer. Winter conditions close the road to all but four-wheel-drive vehicles. Hatchery hours are weekdays, 7:30am to 3:30pm. With prior arrangements the hatchery is open to groups on weekends and holidays.

Directions: *From Pinetop, take Arizona 260 east for four miles to Hon Dah, turn south on Arizona 73 for four miles to Williams Creek Hatchery Road. Turn east and follow the signs for eight miles to the hatchery.*

Ownership: USFWS (334-2346) and (338-4901)
Size: Ninety acres
Closest Town: Pinetop

The large natural springs near the Williams Creek Hatchery form small ponds and marshy areas that attract a variety of wildlife. In Arizona, these marshy areas are often called "cienegas," Spanish for swamp or marsh. JOHN N. CARR

58 POLE KNOLL

Description: This winter cross-country ski recreation area has many trails through Ponderosa pine, mixed conifer and open grassland around a 9,700-foot mountain. Elk, mule deer, wild turkey, Abert and red squirrels, blue grouse, and many songbirds occur here. Songbirds include horned larks, western and mountain bluebirds, western tanagers, red-naped sapsuckers, blue-throated and broad-tailed hummingbirds, and Bewick and winter wrens.

Viewing Information: Trails are marked in reference to cross-country skiing difficulty. Hiking these trails at sunrise or sunset offers the best chance to see many wildlife species. A trail map is located at the parking area on an information board. Best bird viewing is during the migration period in May and June.

Directions: From Eager, go west on Arizona 260 for 13.5 miles to the parking area on the south side of the highway.

Ownership: USFS (333-4372)
Size: 1,200 acres   **Closest Town:** Eager

59 MOUNT BALDY TRAIL

Description: This seven-mile trail follows the West Fork of the Little Colorado River through mountain riparian, old-growth spruce-fir forest, and alpine tundra habitats as it climbs toward the top of Mt. Baldy. Along the trail are outstanding vistas of the surrounding White Mountains. Elk, mule deer, wild turkey, blue grouse, beaver, and spruce-fir forest birds can be seen. Look for songbirds such as the brown creeper, gray-headed junco, Cassin's finch, Virginia's warbler, rufous-sided towhee, mountain bluebirds, and western wood-pewee.

Viewing Information: Sections of the trail pass through the Mt. Baldy Wilderness. The mountain summit is on the White Mountain Apache Reservation and is closed to entry. In late May to October there is an excellent chance to see wildlife along the trail. Severe thunderstorms are common in July and August. A USFS campground is a few miles away from the trailhead.

Directions: From Eager, go west for nineteen miles on Arizona 260, turn south on Arizona 273 for nine miles to the West Fork of the Little Colorado River. Turn right on Forest Road 113J for .5 mile to the trailhead.

Ownership: USFS (333-4372)
Size: Seven-mile trail   **Closest Town:** Eager

60 LEE VALLEY LAKE

Description: This scenic high mountain lake at the foot of Mt. Baldy is the only lake in Arizona with artic grayling. Apache trout are stocked here and are sometimes visible. Surrounding the lake are open meadows and spruce-fir forests. Near the dam, excess water flows through the natural spillway, forming a wetland marsh. Beavers are in Lee Valley Creek upstream from the lake. Birds of the area include osprey, gray jay, blue grouse, broad-tailed and rufous hummingbirds, white-breasted nuthatch, and ruby-crowned kinglet.

Viewing Information: Grayling make their afternoon spawning runs up Lee Valley Creek in early May, the best time to see them. Osprey are often seen perched on nearby snags. Summer is the best time to see birds. A foot trail encircles the lake. A USFS campground is nearby.

Directions: From Eager, go west on Arizona 260 for nineteen miles and turn south on Arizona 273. Continue for eleven miles to Lee Valley Lake.

Ownership: USFS (333-4372)
Size: Fifty acres   **Closest Town:** Eager

The osprey is the only hawk that hovers over water while hunting for fish. Plunging feet-first into the water to catch its prey, the osprey can reverse a "front toe," extending it toward the rear of its foot, thus increasing its grasping ability.
C. ALLAN MORGAN

61 SPRINGERVILLE-BIG LAKE LOOP

Description: This very scenic loop route travels through Ponderosa pine, mixed conifer, mountain meadows, marsh, and riparian habitat, including Salt House Marsh and Mexican Hay Lake, two of the best high-mountain marshes in Arizona. Elk, mule deer, and pronghorn are frequently seen from the road. Other mammals in the area include four species of chipmunks, three species of ground squirrels, and Abert and red squirrels. Mallards, pintails, cinnamon, blue-winged and green-winged teal, canvasbacks, Canada geese, great blue herons, belted kingfishers, red-winged and yellow-headed blackbirds are found in the marsh areas. Western bluebirds and horned larks are common.

Viewing Information: May through October is the best viewing season, with a high probability of seeing many wildlife species. At sunset during spring and summer, there is a high probability of seeing elk at Pat Knoll, ten miles south of Eager. Basin Lake marsh, located a short distance off the route just west of Cresent Lake, is an excellent waterfowl area. Big Lake is a very popular summer recreation area and has complete facilities including a visitor center and a small store.

Directions: *From Eager, go south on Main Street to the sawmill, turning on Water Canyon Road (Forest Road 285). Continue for twenty miles following the signs to Big Lake. Use the paved Arizona 273 and 261 to return to Eager.*

Ownership: USFS (333-4372)
Size: Forty-three-mile route   **Closest Town:** Eager

In spring the marsh habitat of the White Mountains provides nesting areas for many waterfowl, including the cinnamon teal. ART WOLFE

62 LYMAN LAKE STATE PARK

Description: This lake is located at an elevation of 6,000 feet in a mix of pinyon pine, juniper, and open grassland habitats. The dam on the Little Colorado River was built in 1915 and is fed by snowmelt from Mount Baldy and Escudilla Mountain. Waterfowl are common—some species, including Canada geese, nest here in the spring. Snow geese, mallards, pintails, widgeon, and the common merganser frequent the lake. Osprey and bald eagles are also common. A bird list of over 100 species is available. Near the park entrance a small herd of bison is kept in a 180-acre pasture.

Viewing Information: High probability of seeing waterfowl, especially fall through spring. Winter is best for bald eagles. Bison are almost always visible—DO NOT APPROACH BISON. In May barn and cliff swallows build their nests in the picnic ramadas. This park has excellent facilities, including a visitor center and a small store with boat rentals.

Directions: *From St. Johns, go south on U.S. 191 for thirteen miles to the park.*

Ownership: ASP (337-4441)
Size: 1,180 acres   **Closest Town:** St. Johns

63 ESCUDILLA MOUNTAIN-TERRY FLAT

Description: Escudilla Mountain is one of the highest peaks in Arizona at 10,877 feet; most of Terry Flat and the loop road around it are over 9,000 feet. There are old-growth stands of Engleman spruce, Douglas, and white fir in the nearby Escudilla Wilderness Area. Elk, mule deer, wild turkey, blue grouse, black bear, long-tailed weasel, and Abert and red squirrels frequent this area. Sego lily, paint-brush, cinquefoil, and wild onions are among the abundant wildflowers in July and August. Northern goshawks, broad-tailed hummingbirds, gray-headed juncos, western tanagers, and mountain bluebirds are just a few of the many birds seen here.

Viewing Information: May through October there is a high probability of seeing elk, mule deer, and many songbirds. The three-mile trail to the top of the mountain crosses into the wilderness area.

Directions: *From Alpine, go north on U.S. 191 for 5.5 miles, turn onto the Terry Flat-Hulsey Lake Road (Forest Road 56). Continue for about six miles to the beginning of the six-mile loop road around Terry Flat.*

Ownership: USFS (339-4384)
Size: Eighteen-mile loop   **Closest Town:** Alpine

64 LUNA LAKE

Description: This high mountain lake is an excellent site for viewing water-fowl. The upper end of the lake is closed from April to August, providing safe nesting habitat for mallards, cinnamon teal, Canada geese, common cormo-rants, and other waterfowl. The marsh habitat supports muskrats and beaver.

Viewing Information: Beavers and muskrats are best seen in late evening—view from the parking area or from outside the closure fence. Waterfowl are common all year, except when the lake freezes. There is a very nice USFS campground just over a mile past the lake.

Directions: From Alpine, go east on U.S. 180 for four miles to Luna Lake.

Ownership: USFS (339-4384)
Size: 200 acres
Closest Town: Alpine

65 HANNAGAN LOOP

Description: Elk, mule deer, chipmunks, blue grouse, wild turkeys, and Abert and rock squirrels can be seen along this twenty-eight-mile loop. Watch for a variety of forest birds, including western bluebirds, violet-green swallows, yel-low-rumped warblers, and broad-billed hummingbirds. Part of this route passes through a good example of old-growth forest.

Viewing Information: High probability of viewing wildlife along this route, especially in spring and summer. Black bears are here in significant numbers, though seldom seen. Roads are usually not clear of snow until May. The road is gravel but well-maintained over the first twelve miles of the loop; the road becomes rougher over the next ten miles but is passable for all types of ve-hicles in good weather.

Directions: From Alpine, drive south on U.S. 191 for fourteen miles to Buffalo Crossing (Forest Road 26). Turn right and travel about ten miles to Forest Road 24. Turn left and continue for about seven miles to Forest Road 576. Turn left and go four miles to U.S. 191 at Hannagan Meadows. Buffalo Crossing is eight miles north of Hannagan Meadows.

Ownership: USFS (339-4384)
Size: Twenty-eight-mile loop
Closest Town: Alpine

Description: Eagle Creek flows through a well-developed riparian forest, with adjacent grasslands, juniper-oak woodland, and pine on some north-facing slopes. On the road approaching Eagle Creek, watch for two great blue heron rookeries in large cottonwood trees. American kestrels and red-tailed hawks are common and several bald eagles can be seen in winter. Mule deer and white-tailed deer are common in the wooded areas. In winter and spring pronghorn roam the grassland. Other mammals include coyotes, desert cottontails, and chipmunks; birds include northern flickers and several hummingbird species. Rainbow and brown trout are found in Eagle Creek.

Viewing Information: The spring migration period is the best time for viewing birds. The small Honeymoon Campground is at the end of Forest Road 217 which follows Eagle Creek for twelve miles. This graded road can become muddy when wet. Three fords cross Eagle Creek; DO NOT CROSS WHEN FLOODED. Most of the land near Eagle Creek is private property; please respect it. This is a quiet, remote, and uncrowded site.

Directions: From Clifton, take U.S. 191 (Coronado Trail) north for twenty-nine miles to Forest Road 217. Turn west for twenty-two miles to Honeymoon Campground. From the north, Forest Road 217 is forty-three miles south of Hannagan Meadow on U.S. 191.

Ownership: USFS (865-4129)
Size: Ten acres   **Closest Town:** Clifton

The pronghorn is the only member of its biological family, physically different in several ways from other big game animals. Pronghorn have true horns with outer sheaths that are shed annually; they also lack lateral toes, or dew claws.
ERWIN & PEGGY BAUER

67 CORONADO TRAIL

Description: This is a highway to remember. From the high White Mountain town of Springerville to the desert mining town of Clifton, this route passes through spectacular scenic country and offers excellent opportunities to see wildlife. The paved road is open all year, but may close during heavy snow. The route travels through coniferous forest over 9,000 feet to desert scrub at 3,500 feet. Fall colors can be outstanding. Switchbacks and sharp turns along the highway—plan at least six hours for the drive.

Viewing Information: Look for pronghorn in the open grassland around Springerville. Elk can be seen in the forested areas around Alpine and Hannagan Meadow. Active beaver dams are in the creeks along the highway. Blue grouse, Abert and red squirrel, and wild turkeys live in the forested areas. Between Springerville and Alpine is Nelson Reservoir, an excellent site for viewing waterfowl, bald eagles, and osprey. The marshy area at the upper end of the reservoir supports muskrats and waterfowl. Goshawks, bandtail pigeons, and many songbirds can be seen along the way. At its southern end, the highway passes through one of the largest open-pit copper mines in Arizona. Most of this route travels through the Apache National Forest.

Directions: *Start on The Coronado Trail (U.S. 191) at either Clifton or Springerville. It is 123 miles between the two towns.*

Ownership: ADOT, (255-7357); USFS, (333-4301)
Size: 123 miles
Closest Town: Clifton, south;
Springerville, north

Mountain meadows are grassy islands in a sea of trees. Many species of wildlife are attracted to this mix of open space and nutritious vegetation adjacent to the shelter and seeds of the forest. PATRICK FISCHER

68 BONITA CREEK

Description: The scattered stands of large cottonwoods, sycamore, Arizona walnut, ash, and mesquite in this steep-walled canyon are in sharp contrast with the surrounding, rather drab creosote bush desert. Bonita Creek and a portion of the Gila River comprise the Gila Box Riparian National Conservation Area established in 1990. Over 140 species of birds have been recorded here, including black- and zone-tailed hawks, summer tanagers, yellow-billed cuckoos, and Gambel's quail. More than seventy bird species nest along the creek. Mule deer and Rocky Mountain bighorn sheep are in the general area and javelina frequent the canyon bottom. Native fish found in Bonita Creek are the Gila chub, longfin and speckled dace, and Sonoran and mountain suckers.

Viewing Information: Spring and fall are the best viewing times. The probability of seeing birds is highest during the spring migration. Deer and sheep are seldom seen. The road into Bonita Creek follows the north side of the Gila River and crosses several major drainages, which should not be crossed if flooded. A high-clearance vehicle is recommended, especially for the roads leading down into Bonita Creek, which are rocky and steep. There is a four-wheel-drive road in the bottom of Bonita Creek, but it frequently washes out during flood season. USE EXTREME CAUTION. No developed facilities here.

Directions: From Safford, take U.S.70 east for five miles to Solomon, turning north onto Sanchez Road. Cross the Gila River and drive ten miles to a road fork. Turn north and travel five miles to the next junction, taking the right fork one mile to the confluence of Bonita Creek and the Gila River. Follow the left fork, a better road, 1.5 miles to an upstream portion of Bonita Creek.

Ownership: BLM (428-4040)
Size: 500 acres   **Closest Town:** Safford

The large horns of the desert bighorn sheep grow continually and can exceed forty inches in length. During breeding season the growth decreases, causing a ring to form. These growth rings are similar to those in trees, and sheep can be aged by counting them.

REGION 5 - SKY ISLAND MOUNTAINS

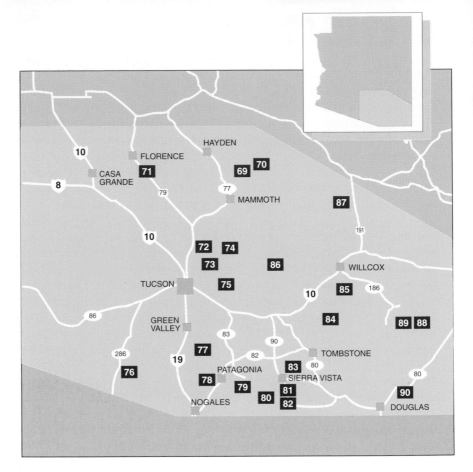

WILDLIFE VIEWING SITES

69 Aravaipa Canyon West

70 Aravaipa Canyon East

71 Pinal Pioneer Parkway

72 Catalina State Park

73 Sabino Canyon Recreation Area

74 Mt. Lemmon (Life Zones)

75 Saguaro National Monument

76 Buenos Aires National
   Wildlife Refuge

77 Madera Canyon

78 Patagonia - Sonoita Creek Preserve

79 Bog Hole Wildlife Area

80 Parker Canyon Lake

81 Ramsey Canyon Preserve

82 Carr Canyon - The Reef

83 San Pedro Riparian National
   Conservation Area

84 Cochise Stronghold East

85 Willcox Playa Wildlife Area

86 Muleshoe Ranch Management Area

87 Swift Trail (Life Zones)

88 Cave Creek Canyon Recreation Area

89 Rustler Park Recreation Area

90 Chiricahua Trail

Description: Aravaipa Creek flows west through the Galiuro Mountains to meet the San Pedro River. The access road to the trailhead follows Aravaipa Canyon to the beginning of the Wilderness. Most of the canyon bottom land is private. The George Whittell Wildlife Preserve, at the canyon entrance, is a project of The Nature Conservancy and Defenders of Wildlife to preserve this valuable wildlife habitat. Seven species of native Arizona fish occur in Aravaipa Creek, including two sucker species, longfin dace, speckled dace, spikedace, loach minnow, and roundtail chub. Toads, frogs, turtles, and the desert tortoise are found here. Side-blotched and tree lizards are among the twenty species recorded here.

Viewing Information: These small fish are seen in the shaded, protected pools. This site is only eleven miles from Aravaipa Canyon East, but 170 miles by road. Check the information listed under Aravaipa Canyon East for hiking permits and other wildlife.

Directions: From Mammoth, go eight miles north on Arizona 77 to Aravaipa Canyon Road. Continue for 12 miles to the trailhead.

Ownership: BLM (428-4040)
Size: 1,200 acres
Closest Town: Mammoth

The great diversity of vegetation within Aravaipa Canyon creates habitats for over 300 species of fish, reptiles, amphibians, birds, and mammals. The canyon, part of the National Wilderness System, provides protection for habitat and wildlife and solitude for visitors.
JACK W. DYKINGA

73

70 ARAVAIPA CANYON EAST

Description: Aravaipa Canyon is one of the jewels of the Southwest. It offers spectacular scenery with giant sycamore, cottonwood, and ash trees. Aravaipa Creek begins in a broad valley; as it enters the Galiuro Mountains, the canyon walls rise over a thousand feet to form a narrow gorge. Over 230 bird species have been recorded here, including black- and zone-tailed hawks, blue grosbeaks, and yellow warblers. White-tailed deer, mule deer, javelina, bighorn sheep, coatimundi, gray fox, and raccoons are common. In 1969 the canyon became BLM's first Primitive Area and in 1984 the Aravaipa Canyon Wilderness was created. The Nature Conservancy owns the last five miles of the canyon bottom to the trailhead. A checklist of all vertebrate species is available.

Viewing Information: The chance of seeing wildlife is high. Viewing must be done from the road as no access is permitted into the private property. The trailhead at the end of the road is public land. The road crosses the creek several times—DO NOT CROSS WHEN FLOODED. Only fifty people per day (twenty on east trailhead and thirty from the west) are allowed to hike the eleven miles through the canyon and fee permits are required well in advance. There is a BLM campground at Klondyke.

Directions: *Take Arizona 70 fifteen miles northwest of Safford to Klondyke Road. Go forty-five miles west through Klondyke and then ten miles to the east trailhead.*

Ownership: TNC, (828-3443); BLM, (428-4040)
Size: 1,200 acres
Closest Town: Safford

Desert bighorn sheep prefer the hot, dry desert mountains of western and central Arizona. In a few areas, research biologists have placed radio collars or ear tags on bighorn sheep to study life histories and the animals' patterns of movement.

BOB MILES

Description: This thirty-mile route passes through classic Sonoran Desert upland habitat. At the south end there are a few miles of desert grassland with prickly pear cactus and small bushes. Traveling north, the desert becomes heavily vegetated with ironwood, paloverde and mesquite trees, and many saguaros and cholla cactus. The understory is dominated by grey-green bur sage. Wildlife here is typical of the Sonoran Desert. This scenic highway has a low volume of traffic. A pleasant and leisurely alternate route between Tucson and Phoenix; about halfway along the route is the Tom Mix Monument.

Viewing Information: Spring offers the best viewing. When winter moisture is above normal, desert flower displays can be fantastic and the highway will be lined with blue lupine intermixed with yellow flowers of brittle-bush and California poppies. Ironwood trees have lavendar flowers and paloverde flowers are yellow. In April, the male Gambel's quail may be seen on a high perch; listen for his single-note mating call. Look into the chain fruit cholla for the cactus wren building nests in this spiny protective cover. Early in the morning, blacktail or the white-sided antelope jackrabbits may be seen. Meadowlarks, phainopepla, curved-bill thrashers and red-tailed hawks are common. Park in the turnouts or one of five picnic areas. Use binoculars to look at the saguaros and the nesting holes excavated by Gila Woodpeckers and gilded flickers.

Directions: *This route on Arizona 79 is between the towns of Florence and Oracle Junction.*

Ownership: ADOT (255-7357)
Size: Thirty miles
Closest town: Florence, north; Oracle Junction, south

The Gambel's quail is widely distributed in Arizona, from very dry desert to pinyon pine-juniper habitats. Above average winter and spring rainfall stimulates reproduction, producing larger coveys. LARRY R. DITTO

72 CATALINA STATE PARK

Description: This park is in the floodplain of Canyon del Oro north of the Santa Catalina Mountains. There is an excellent example of a mature mesquite bosque surrounded by Sonoran Desert with paloverde trees and saguaro cactus. Desert bighorn sheep live in the rugged area of Pusch Ridge. Mule deer, red-tailed hawks, Gambel's quail, cactus wrens, and Gila woodpeckers are common. Collared and whiptail lizards are easily seen in the warmer months.

Viewing Information: The park is the starting point for two long trails, Romero Canyon and Sutherland Trail, both of which lead to the top of the Santa Catalina Mountains, with a summit of 9,000 feet. The park has an equestrian center and trails. The cooler months are best for wildlife viewing.

Directions: Located fourteen miles north of downtown Tucson on Arizona 77. Entrance is six miles north of the junction of Ina Road and Arizona 77.

Ownership: USFS; ASP (628-5798)
Size: 5,500 acres
Closest Town: Tucson

73 SABINO CANYON RECREATION AREA

Description: This site is located at the foot of the Santa Catalina Mountains in the Sonoran Desert. The riparian habitat and flowing stream in this canyon setting are very popular with residents of nearby Tucson. Near the visitor center are Gambel's quail, roadrunners, roundtail ground squirrel, and Harris antelope ground squirrels. In the canyon, look for Anna's hummingbirds, cardinals, hooded orioles, ringtails, and collared lizards.

Viewing Information: Vehicle travel is restricted; a shuttle bus (fee required) provides access to Upper Sabino and adjacent Bear Canyon. Trails also provide access to Upper Sabino and the higher parts of the canyon, and into the mountain. Even though this is a high-use area, wildlife viewing is excellent. There are guided nature and bird walks almost every day, especially in winter. The visitor center contains many exhibits and interpretive information.

Directions: From Tucson, take Sunrise Road in the Catalina Foothills and go east to Sabino Canyon Road. Turn north; first right is the Sabino Canyon visitor center.

Ownership: USFS (749-8700)
Size: 2,800 acres
Closest Town: Tucson

Description: The Santa Catalina Mountains rise abruptly from the desert floor to 9,157 feet at Mount Lemmon. The General Hitchcock Highway goes through a series of Life Zone classifications: Lower Sonoran, desert; Upper Sonoran, woodlands; Transition, coniferous forest; Canadian, spruce-fir forest; and a unique remnant cypress forest. As the vegetation changes so does the wildlife, with Gambel's quail and cactus wrens in the desert; Mexican jays, Montezuma quail, and white-tail deer in the woodland; bandtail pigeons, Merriam's turkey, and Abert squirrels in the Ponderosa pine; and black bear, Mexican spotted owls, and goshawks in the fir forest. All of these changes occur along this forty mile route.

Viewing Information: There are many parking areas, vistas and campgrounds along the paved highway, and these are the best places to look for wildlife. The visitor center at the Palisades Ranger Station has excellent interpretive information about wildlife and life zones. At Summerhaven, several commercial establishments have feeders that attract many hummingbirds, including black-chinned, rufous, broad-tailed, magnificent, and Anna's. In winter, heavy snows can temporarily close the highway.

Directions: *From Tucson, go east on Speedway Boulevard to Wilmot Road, then turn north following the curve. Here it becomes Tanque Verde Road. Go about four miles to the Catalina Highway (also known as the General Hitchcock Highway).*

Owner: USFS (749-8700)
Size: Forty miles
Closest Town: Tucson

A resident of the Ponderosa pine forest, the Abert or tassel-eared squirrel grows long tufts of hair on the ears in late fall and winter. BOB MILES

LIFE ZONES

At the turn of the century many biologist-explorers came to Arizona to study this new land and its wildlife. The work of one scientist, Dr. C. Hart Merriam, shed light on the ways that plants and animals develop into distinct communities. Merriam called these communities *Life Zones*, and identified six distinct zones based on his studies in Arizona. One hundred years later, Dr. Merriam's Life Zone concepts are still used by biologists the world over.

Life Zones refer to the consistent pattern of changes that occur in plantlife through changes in elevation and latitude. Temperature and moisture are two factors that dictate the changes in each Life Zone. These factors and the vegetative composition determine the kinds of wildlife that live in each habitat. Beginning at the lowest elevation, Merriam's Life Zones are:

1. **Lower Sonoran.** The hot deserts.

2. **Upper Sonoran.** The grasslands, chaparral, woodlands.

One of Arizona's "sky island mountains," the Pinaleno Mountains rise to 10,000 feet above the desert floor. Four distinct Life Zones—unique communities of plants and animals—can be found in a trip from desert to mountaintop. BOB MILES

3. Transition. Pine trees.

4. Canadian. Douglas-fir and Engleman spruce.

5. Hudsonian. Fir forest.

6. Alpine tundra, above the timber line.

Life Zones are particularly useful in describing habitat types in the Southwest, where many mountains rise abruptly from the desert floor to elevations above 9,000 feet. The Mount Lemmon and Swift Trail viewing sites in this guide (sites 74 and 87) best demonstrate the Life Zone concept. Their changing vegetation and the corresponding wildlife composition are easily and dramatically seen. These changes, evident in a short thirty-mile drive up the mountains, are comparable to driving from the Arizona desert to the spruce forest of Montana.

Found only in the Pinaleno Mountains, the endangered Mount Graham red squirrel lives in the spruce-fir forest of the Canadian Life Zone. BOB MILES

75 SAGUARO NATIONAL PARK

Description: There are two districts in this national monument, east of Tucson in the Rincon Mountains and west in the Tucson Mountains. Both areas contain magnificent stands of the giant saguaro cactus and excellent viewing opportunities to see Sonoran Desert wildlife. On the desert floor are javelina and mule deer. Desert tortoise, Gila monsters, and western diamondback rattlesnakes are relatively common in this desert habitat.

Viewing Information: The interpretive information about desert wildlife is excellent. Many animals depend on the saguaro cactus; the numerous holes excavated by gilded flickers and Gila woodpeckers provide homes and nests for elf and screech owls, cactus wrens, and Lucy's warblers. The white-winged dove feeds on the saguaro seeds, and longnose bats pollinate the saguaro flowers as they feed on the nectar. The east district has trails to the top of the Rincon Mountains that reach an elevation of 9,000 feet. Backcountry permits are required.

Directions: Both districts are about fifteen miles from downtown Tucson. To reach Saguaro East, take Broadway Road east to Old Spanish Trail and follow signs to the entrance. To reach Saguaro West, take Speedway Boulevard west over Gates Pass and follow the signs to the entrance.

Ownership: NPS (Saguaro West 883-6366 / Saguaro East 296-8576)
Size: 87,114 acres
Closest Town: Tucson

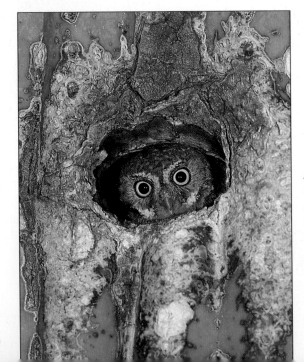

About the size of a sparrow, the elf owl nests in abandoned holes in Saguaro cactus that were excavated by Gila woodpeckers or gilded flickers. Their high-pitched twittering on a descending scale is one of the common night sounds of the desert. BRYAN MUNN

Description: This refuge was established in 1985 to preserve desert grassland habitat and to reintroduce the endangered masked bobwhite quail in Altar Valley, about seventy miles southwest of Tucson. It is the only place in the United States where four species of quail occur: the Gambel's quail, scale quail, Montezuma quail, and masked bobwhite may all be seen here. The refuge elevation ranges from 3,200 to 4,800 feet. The Arivaca Cienega, Spanish for marsh or swamp, is on the east side of the refuge and has an outstanding mature cottonwood riparian area, excellent for birds.

Viewing Information: A checklist of the site's 239 recorded bird species is available. Some subtropical birds breed here, including the rose-throated becard. Also look for pronghorn, mule deer, javelina, jack rabbits, and coyotes. A self-guided ten-mile auto tour is open from daylight to dark all year. REFUGE ROADS CAN BE VERY MUDDY AFTER RAINS.

Directions: *From Tucson, take Arizona 86 (Ajo Way) west to Robles Junction. Turn south on Arizona 286 for thirty-eight miles to the refuge entrance. To go to the Arivaca Cienega, take Arizona 289 east from the refuge for twelve miles to the town of Arivaca. Go south on the Ruby Road for a short distance to a parking area. Another access to Arivaca Cienega and Buenos Aries Refuge is from I-19 at Exit 48 (Arivaca Jct.): go west for twenty-four miles to Arivaca.*

Ownership: USFWS (823-4251)
Size: 114,000 acres   **Closest Town:** Sasabe

Biologists refer to the vegetation of Altar Valley as the Sonoran savannah grasslands. Efforts are underway to re-establish the endangered masked bobwhite quail in this historic habitat. JACK W. DYKINGA

77 MADERA CANYON

Description: This canyon in the Santa Rita Mountains adjacent to the desert contains a rare combination of climate, vegetation, and elevation changes that produce unique conditions for wildlife. The Santa Ritas are one of the "sky islands" of southeastern Arizona, rising to 9,324 feet at Mount Wrightson. Madera Canyon, an excellent example of oak woodland and riparian habitat, is well-known for its birds. Along with fifteen species of hummingbirds, watch for the elegant trogon, sulphur-bellied flycatcher, and flammulated owl. The trailhead at the end of the paved road leads to the top of the mountain. White-tailed deer, javelina, Arizona gray squirrel, and coatimundi are also in the area.

Viewing Information: A bird checklist is available; over 200 species have been recorded at this site. Birding season begins in early March with the arrival of hummingbirds and owls. The best time to see the Coues white-tailed deer is in December and January. There are numerous nature trails, including a handicap trail in the lower canyon. At the Santa Rita Lodge, many hummingbirds are attracted to feeders. The lodge also sponsors a series of nature programs with reservations required. There are limited cabins and early reservations are necessary.

Directions: *From Green Valley on Interstate 19, take Exit 63 and drive east past the Continental School. Continue east on Forest Road 62 for nine miles to the junction of Forest Road 70. Follow Forest Road 70 to Madera Canyon.*

Ownership: USFS, (281-2296); Santa Rita Lodge, (625-8746)
Size: 640 acres
Closest Town: Green Valley

More hummingbird species are found in southeastern Arizona mountain canyons than in any other place in the United States. The broad-billed hummingbird is one of fifteen species that occur in Madera Canyon.
C. ALLAN MORGAN

78 | PATAGONIA - SONOITA CREEK PRESERVE

Description: An outstanding example of riparian woodland habitat and one of the best-known birding spots in the state, this site is a registered National Natural Landmark dominated by giant Fremont cottonwood, willow, velvet ash, and Arizona walnut trees. More than 250 bird and 300 plant species have been recorded here. Gray hawks, vermilion flycatchers, and many warblers are commonly seen here. Blue herons nest in the giant cottonwood trees at the eastern end of the Preserve.

Viewing Information: A weekly bird sighting checklist is posted on the entrance bulletin board. Access trails wind through the riparian area and along Sonoita Creek. April through September is the best viewing period. A visitor center and other facilities are scheduled for construction in late 1992. The preserve is open from 7:30 am to 3:30 pm Wednesday through Sunday.

Directions: *From Arizona 82 in Patagonia, turn west at 4th Avenue, turn south at Pennsylvania Avenue and follow the gravel road for one mile to the Preserve entrance. DO NOT CROSS SONOITA CREEK IF FLOODED.*

Ownership: TNC (394-2400)
Size: 350 acres   **Closest Town:** Patagonia

79 | BOG HOLE WILDLIFE AREA

Description: This six-acre pond was built to provide habitat for the mallard-like Mexican duck and other waterfowl. The surrounding grasslands of San Rafael Valley open unexpectedly from the oak-covered hills and canyons. The Sprague's pipit and Baird's sparrow, also pronghorn, are found in the open shortgrass prairie. White-tailed deer and javelina are in the wooded areas. Montezuma quail are common in the oak woodlands but are difficult to see.

Viewing Information: Bald eagles and waterfowl use the area in winter. Pronghorn are almost always seen. There are no facilities at this site. The roads can be muddy and impassable after heavy rains or winter snow. A high-clearance vehicle is recommended for the last half-mile of the drive.

Directions: *From Patagonia, take Forest Road 58 east for ten miles and turn north on Forest Road 765 (Meadow Valley Road). Continue two miles (keep to the right after crossing a cattleguard) to a two-track road, turn right and continue .5 mile.*

Ownership: USFS, (378-0311); AGFD, (628-5376)
Size: 200 acres   **Closest Town:** Patagonia

80 PARKER CANYON LAKE

Description: Located in the oak woodland foothills of the Huachuca Mountains and near the shortgrass prairie of San Rafael Valley, this site offers a mix of habitat types and a variety of viewing opportunities. The eighty-acre lake is a popular recreation area and attracts bald eagles, osprey, and waterfowl in winter. White-tailed deer, javelina, Montezuma quail, and Arizona gray squirrels are all fairly common in this area.

Viewing Information: Observation points along a five-mile trail around the lake provide the best opportunity to see wildlife. On the drive from Sonoita there is a good chance to view deer and pronghorn. This is one of the best areas to see the coatimundi, a raccoon-like neighbor from Mexico. The Huachuca Mountains are home to the rare and protected Willard's and twin spotted rattlesnakes.

Directions: *From Sonoita, drive thirty miles southeast on Arizona 83. The last twenty miles are unpaved.*

Ownership: USFS (378-0311)
Size: 300 acres   **Closest Town:** Sonoita

The coatimundi is related to the raccoon and found in the woodlands of southeastern Arizona. Locally they are sometimes called "chulo bears." BOB MILES

81 RAMSEY CANYON PRESERVE

Description: The preserve is located in the middle elevations of Ramsey Canyon, a steep-sided, heavily wooded canyon on the east side of the Huachuca Mountains. Vegetation includes pine-oak woodland and sycamore-maple riparian forest. The site is well-known for its variety of plant and animal life, particularly birds, butterflies and reptiles. Arizona gray squirrels, Coues' whitetail deer and coatimundi are common. Its international reputation and accessibility make this one of The Nature Conservancy's most popular preserves. The site is small, and access is limited to protect fragile habitats and sensitive wildlife. Carr Canyon, one mile south, is an excellent alternate site. Reservations are required for weekends and holidays. Large vehicles or those pulling trailers cannot be accommodated due to the narrow loop driveway. The Nature Conservancy rents six cabins at the site, but reservations may be necessary well in advance. The preserve has two self-guiding trails, a visitor center with bookstore and native flower gardens.

Viewing Information: Best viewing times are spring through fall with a high probability of viewing most species May through September. Songbird migration peaks in late April, hummingbird numbers and diversity peak in August. Wildflowers, butterflies and reptiles are easily seen August through October. Mammal activity is highest in fall and winter. Trail guides and wildlife checklists are available.

Directions: *From Sierra Vista take Arizona 92 south for six miles. Turn west on Ramsey Canyon Road for four miles to the preserve entrance.*

Ownership: TNC (378-2785)
Size: 300 acres **Closest Town:** Sierra Vista

Hummingbirds have developed a hovering type of flight in order to feed on the nectar of brightly colored tubular flowers. The flowers in turn are pollinated by the feeding hummingbirds. Each has evolved to attract the other to maintain the benefits of this relationship. A male broad-tailed hummingbird can be identified as it flies through the forest by the shrill trilling sound made by its wings.

82 CARR CANYON - THE REEF

Description: The Huachuca Mountains are one of the "sky island" mountains in southeastern Arizona, rising to 9,466 feet at Miller Peak. In the 1970's, several large fires burned extensive areas of the mountain. While the fire scars are evident, the openness provides excellent opportunities for wildlife viewing, as well as a firsthand look at forest vegetation recovery. White-tailed deer, Arizona gray squirrel, golden eagle, Strickland's woodpecker, olive and red-faced warblers may be seen. Black bears are in the higher elevations.

Viewing Information: A trip to The Reef above Carr Canyon starts in grassland, through oak woodland and a streamside riparian area. The narrow, twisting mountain road provides the only vehicle access to The Reef's pine forest. Several vista points provide outstanding views of the ribbon of green riparian habitat along the San Pedro River in the valley below. Hummingbirds are abundant during August and September. This site can be an alternate to Ramsey Canyon, a mile to the north, which has very limited parking space. Winter snows may close access to The Reef.

Directions: *From Sierra Vista, take Arizona 92 south for seven miles, turn west on Carr Canyon Road and continue for eight miles to the end of the road and the trail access points.*

Ownership: USFS (378-0311)
Size: Eight-mile route
Closest Town: Sierra Vista

The elegant trogon is a brightly-colored tropical bird that nests in southeastern Arizona. They will be found in canyons of the Huachuca, Santa Rita and Chiricahua Mountains.
PAT O'BRIEN

Description: The San Pedro River is managed to preserve this sensitive ecosystem dominated by Fremont cottonwoods and Gooding willows. Other bottom lands have mesquite bosques and dense stands of sacaton grass. The upland areas are Chihuahuan Desert scrub, typified by short thorny plants, creosote, and tarbush. The river once supported fourteen species of native fish, but only the longfin dace and desert sucker remain. While mule deer and javelina are common, the area is best known for birds: 379 species have been recorded, 100 of which nest here. The thirty-five species of raptors include gray and Swainson's hawks, Mississippi kite, and crested caracara. The Sonoran box turtle and Couch's spadefoot toad are common. The western diamondback and Mojave rattlesnakes are found here, so be careful, especially during the warm months.

Viewing Information: One of the outstanding wildlife viewing areas in southeastern Arizona, with plenty of room and uncrowded conditions. The Conservation Area extends upstream from the Mexican border for forty miles. Park at any access point and walk up or down the river for best viewing opportunities. March through September offer the highest probability of seeing birds; a bird checklist is available. BLM Headquarters is open weekdays, San Pedro House on weekends. Picnic facilities are available only at the San Pedro House. Back country camping is allowed; check at BLM headquarters for permit and fee.

Directions: There are six easy access points to the San Pedro River: Land Corral south of St. David; Arizona 82 at Fairbank (BLM Headquarters); Charleston Road; Hereford Road; Arizona 92; and Arizona 90 (San Pedro House). All access points are east of Sierra Vista.

Ownership: BLM (457-2265)
Size: 56,500 acres   **Closest Town:** Sierra Vista

The desert box turtle has the ability to completely enclose its feet, tail and head within its "box" shell. This largely terrestrial turtle prefers gently rolling open country, but occasionally enters the water.
RANDALL D. BABB

84 COCHISE STRONGHOLD EAST

Description: This rugged canyon with large granite boulders was once the home of Cochise, the legendary Apache chief. A seasonal stream here is bordered by sycamore, walnut, hackberry, willow and Arizona cypress trees, which shelter many birds. Mexican jays, black-chinned hummingbirds, prairie falcons, turkey vultures, and golden eagles can be seen, especially in late spring and summer. Mule deer are found in the lower elevation grassland area; white-tailed deer inhabit the woodlands. The boulders make this an excellent place for bobcats, coatimundi and ringtails.

Viewing Information: Along the road are areas of private property. There is a short nature trail from the campground, as well as longer trails into the Dragoon Mountains and to the West Stronghold. The West site is more remote with no facilities and can be accessed from Tombstone via Middlemarch Road and Forest Road 687. Similar wildlife may be seen in both areas.

Directions: *From Interstate 10 (Exit 331), go south on U.S. 191 18 miles to Sunsites. Turn west on Ironwood Road and go 10 miles to the site.*

Ownership: USFS (364-3468)
Size: 200 acres   **Closest Town:** Sunsites

85 WILLCOX PLAYA WILDLIFE AREA

Description: This site is located on the northeast side of the Willcox Playa, a 37,000-acre enclosed drainage basin in Sulphur Springs Valley that appears as a dry lake bed. Around the perimeter, especially on the north end, are depressions and ponds. In the rainy seasons the Playa may be filled with several inches of water. More than 6,000 sandhill cranes winter here. The farms in the area provide food for cranes and waterfowl. The entire valley is an excellent area to view hawks in winter. Gambel's and scale quail are also present.

Viewing Information: Fire breaks in the Wildlife Area can be used as access trails for viewing. High probability of seeing sandhill cranes in winter. Birds use the Playa for roosting and leave very early in the morning to feed in neighboring farms, sometimes traveling as far as Bonita, forty miles to the north.

Directions: *From Willcox, go east on Arizona 186 for six miles, turn south on the Kansas Settlement Road for four miles to the Wildlife Area.*

Ownership: AGFD (628-5376)
Size: 550 acres   **Closest Town:** Willcox

Description: This area is jointly managed by The Nature Conservancy, BLM and USFS to conserve and enhance a unique Arizona ecosystem. The ranch contains a wide variety of habitats, from desert to Ponderosa pine. Six perennial streams provide habitat for five native fish; Gila chub, long fin dace, speckled dace and two suckers. Parts of the ranch are extremely rugged and home to desert big horn sheep, white-tailed deer and mountain lions. Smaller mammals include raccoons, coatimundi and javelina. Two hundred bird species regularly occur here and include zone-tailed, black and gray hawks, western tanager, hooded oriole and acorn woodpecker. This is a remote and quiet area away from crowds. It provides a unique opportunity for viewing wildlife.

Viewing Information: Access to the ranch headquarters is via a graded road that can be hazardous when wet. Cars can drive to the ranch but the fourteen mile Jackson Cabin Road to the Galiuro and Redfield Canyon Wilderness Areas is four-wheel-drive vehicles only. All visitors should register at the information board. Guided horseback trips are available in April and October with advance reservations. Accommodations at the ranch headquarters are limited and require reservations. Species lists and interpretive information about the Cooperative Management Area are available at the headquarters.

Directions: *From Willcox, go west on Airport Road for fifteen miles to Muleshoe Ranch turn-off, turn north and continue fifteen miles to end of the road.*

Ownership: TNC, (586-7072); BLM, (428-4040); USFS, (428-4150)
Size: 49,000 acres
Closest Town: Willcox

Springtime in the rugged Galiuro Mountains offers opportunities to see desert wildflowers, riparian birds, and other wildlife. JACK W. DYKINGA

87 SWIFT TRAIL/LIFE ZONES

Description: The Swift Trail (Arizona 366) reaches nearly to the top of the Pinaleno Mountains and Mount Graham, the highest peak in southern Arizona at 10,720 feet. This site is an excellent opportunity to experience Arizona's series of Life Zones—from the desert floor to the forest of Engleman spruce and corkbark fir. Lower Sonoran, desert habitat of prickly pear cactus and ocotillo with collared lizards, roadrunners, and cactus wrens occurs in the first three miles. The next several miles change to Upper Sonoran Life Zone, a woodland of oak, juniper, and manzanita inhabited by rock squirrels, cliff chipmunks, gray-breasted jays, and red-tailed hawks. The next ten miles is mixed conifer habitat, the Transition Zone, with bandtail pigeons, scrub jays, and northern flickers. During June and July, millions of ladybugs cover everything at Ladybug Saddle. From Hospital Flat until the road ends is a mixture of Ponderosa pine, aspen, white and corkbark fir with hummingbirds in summer, pine sisken, white-bellied voles, black bear, Abert squirrel, white-tailed deer, yellow-eyed junco, brown creepers and the endangered Mount Graham red squirrel. The Canadian Zone is represented by white and corkbark fir. Gold Apache trout are found in Grant and Ash Creeks; rainbow trout are in Riggs Flat Lake.

Viewing Information: It is an eighty-five-mile round-trip from Safford with a minimum driving time of five hours. The Safford Ranger District has an automobile tour guide and trail information. There are many picnic and camping areas and a visitors center at Columbine (open after April 15). The last eleven miles are not paved and are closed from November 15 to April 15.

Directions: *From Safford, take U.S. 191 south for 8 miles to Arizona 366 (Swift Trail Junction).*

Ownership: USFS (428-4150)
Size: Thirty-five-mile route
Closest Town: Safford

Spadefoot toads bury themselves deep into the ground and emerge when summer rains create pools. They come out, take a mate, and the young hatch in thirty-six hours and grow to young spadefoots in ten to fifteen days. These young adults will then bury themselves as the life cycle begins again.

Description: Scientists at the nearby Southwest Research Station say that Cave Creek Canyon has the richest diversity of wildlife in the United States. This is a unique area with climactic influence from the Chihuahuan Desert, subtropical habitats of Mexico, Sonoran Desert, and mountain habitats of North America. This mix attracts hundreds of bird species. A program is underway here to reintroduce the thick-billed parrot, the only parrot native to North America. The reddish Chiricahua fox squirrel is only found in the Chiricahua Mountains. White-tailed deer, javelina, ringtail cats, black bears, peregrine falcons, cooper's hawks, elegant trogons, painted redstarts, sulphur-bellied flycatchers, blue-throated and magnificent hummingbirds are just a few of the wildlife species found here.

Viewing Information: Spring and summer are the best times to see birds, though birding is good year-round. Fall colors can be brilliant from the sycamore, maple, and ash trees mixed in with the evergreen Arizona cypress and the long-needled Apache pines. The South Fork Zoological Botanical Area is a special area set aside for wildlife study and viewing.

Directions: *From Portal take Forest Road 42 west for one mile into the Coronado National Forest and continue past the visitor center to the camping and parking areas.*

Ownership: USFS (364-3468)
Size: Six-mile route   **Closest Town:** Portal

Efforts are underway to reintroduce the thick-billed parrot to its original habitat in southeastern Arizona. This bird is a resident of pine forests, and feeds on pine cones, cracking them open with its powerful bill. BOB MILES

89 RUSTLER PARK RECREATION AREA

Description: At 8,500 feet, this mountain meadow campgound is nestled in pine-fir forest. A few miles away by trail is the 9,795-foot-high Chiricahua Peak. This area features the southernmost stand of Engleman spruce, as well as iris and orchids that attract many butterflies and hummingbirds in summer. Mexican chickadees, yellow-eyed junco, pygmy nuthatch, and hairy woodpeckers are a few of the birds seen here. Black bear and mountain lion are common but difficult to see. Bunch-grass lizards and the rare twin-spotted rattlesnake may also be seen.

Viewing Information: Walking the trails in the early morning is the best way to see white-tailed deer. In spring and summer there is a high probability of viewing high-elevation bird species. Access from the west past the Chiricahua National Monument through Pinery Canyon or from the east through Cave Creek Canyon is an exciting trip on a narrow, twisting mountain road. Winter snows will close the road. USE CAUTION WHEN THE ROAD IS WET.

Directions: *From Portal, go west on Forest Road 42 for about twelve miles to Onion Saddle. Turn south on Forest Road 42D for three miles to the campground. From Willcox, go east on Arizona 186 for thirty-five miles to Chiricahua National Monument entrance, then turn southeast on Forest Road 42 for twelve miles to Onion Saddle. Follow the signs to Rustler Park campground.*

Ownership: USFS (364-3468)
Size: Thirty acres
Closest Town: Portal

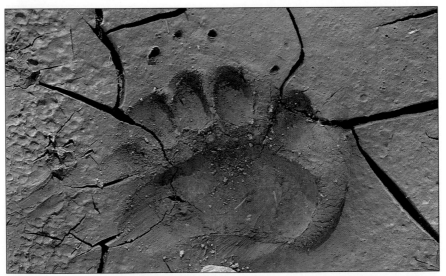

Black bears are shy and secretive like many wild animals, and not often seen. A bear track in the mud can be an exciting reminder that these large mammals are in the area

Description: This fifty-mile stretch of Arizona 80 crosses the extreme southeastern corner of the state, passing near the Perrilla, Pedregosa and Chiricahua Mountains. The route is close to Skeleton Canyon, where the famous Apache Chief Geronimo surrendered to American troops in 1877. Near Douglas, the Chihuahuan Desert is dominated by white thorn, shrubby mesquite, yucca and creosote bush. Javelina and mule deer are found in the nearby hills. Scale quail, roadrunners, Scott's oriole, and curved-bill thrasher are a few of the common birds. Kestrels, prairie falcons, harriers, and red-tailed hawks can often be seen from the highway. This area is well known for reptiles—collared lizards, Mexican blackheaded snakes, horned lizards and eight species of rattlesnakes, including the massasauga, occur here.

Viewing Information: April through September is the best season to see reptiles. Nectar feeding bats frequent the area in May when yucca plants are flowering. In the open grasslands of the San Bernadino Valley, near the smooth cinder cone hills, there is a moderate probability to see pronghorn and grassland sparrows. No facilities along this route.

Directions: *This fifty-mile route is between Douglas, Arizona, and Rodeo, New Mexico on Arizona 80.*

Ownership: ADOT (255-7357)
Size: Fifty miles   **Closest Town:** Douglas

When running at high speed, the collared lizard sometimes runs upright on its hind legs. An excellent jumper, this aggressive lizard will bite if captured. DAVED W. LAZAROFF

POPULAR WILDLIFE VIEWING SPECIES OF ARIZONA
—AND WHERE TO FIND THEM

The index below identifies some of the more interesting, uncommon, or attractive wildlife found in Arizona, and some of the best sites for viewing selected species. Many of the animals listed may be viewed at other sites as well. The numbers following each species are site numbers, not page numbers.

BIRDS
MARINE BIRDS
Pelican 19, 22, 23, 26

BIRDS OF PREY
Bald eagle 7-9, 17, 19, 26, 35, 39, 41, 42, 47, 48, 57, 60, 62, 67, 80
Black hawk 27, 40, 41, 68
Golden eagle 4, 6, 12, 21, 27, 82
Goshawk 1, 58, 63
Gray hawk 28, 68, 78, 83, 86
Harris hawk 25, 29, 47-49
Kestrel and prairie falcon 6, 11, 12, 34, 37, 66
Osprey 7-9, 17, 19, 26, 35, 39, 41, 42, 47, 48, 57, 60, 62, 67, 80
Zone-tailed hawk 28, 68, 78, 83, 86

SONGBIRDS
American dipper 43, 46, 57, 59
Hummingbirds 44, 46, 52, 54, 58, 60, 63, 65, 66, 73, 74, 77, 81, 82, 84, 88, 89
Trogon 77, 81, 82, 88
Yellow-billed cuckoo 39, 51, 68, 83
Western bluebird 46, 61, 63, 65
Desert birds 21, 27, 29, 32, 49, 52, 71, 72, 75, 76
Mountain birds 1, 2, 7-10, 14, 17, 33, 35, 38, 44, 54, 57-60, 63, 65, 74, 77, 82, 83, 89
Riparian Birds 20, 25, 28, 30, 32, 39, 40-43, 46-48, 50, 51, 53, 66, 68-70, 73, 78, 81, 83, 86, 88

UPLAND BIRDS
Blue grouse 2, 58-60, 63, 65
Gambel quail 19, 22, 23, 30, 34, 39, 42, 48, 49, 52, 72, 73, 76, 90
Masked bobwhite quail 76
Montezuma quail 76, 79, 80
Scale quail 76, 84, 85, 90
Wild turkey 1, 7, 8, 10, 33, 38, 45, 46, 59, 65, 67, 82

WADING BIRDS
Egrets and heron 19, 20, 22-26, 28, 35, 42, 47, 48, 51, 66, 78
Sandhill crane 22, 85

WATERFOWL
Canada geese and snow geese 19, 22, 23, 51, 61, 62, 64,
Ducks 7, 9, 15, 17, 19, 20, 22, 23, 24, 26, 27, 35, 36, 55, 56, 61, 62, 64, 79

FISH
Native fish 27, 28, 32, 50, 52, 57, 68-70, 86

WHERE THE WILD THINGS ARE

Falcon Press puts wildlife viewing secrets at your fingertips with our high-quality, full color guidebooks—the Watchable Wildlife Series. This is the only official series of guides for the National Watchable Wildlife Program: areas featured in the books correspond to official sites across America. And you'll find more than just wildlife. Many sites boast beautiful scenery, interpretive displays, opportunities for hiking, picnics, biking, plus—a little peace and quiet. So pick up one of our Wildlife Viewing Guides today and get close to Mother Nature!

WATCH THIS
PARTNERSHIP WORK

The National Watchable Wildlife Program was formed with one goal in mind: get people actively involved in wildlife appreciation and conservation. Defenders of Wildlife has led the way by coordinating this unique multi-agency program and developing a national network of prime wildlife viewing areas.

Part of the proceeds go to conserve wildlife and wildlife habitat.

Visit your local bookstore for more information or call toll-free for a free catalog of nature-related books and gift ideas.

1-800-582-2665
Falcon Press
P.O. Box 1718
Helena, MT 59624